THEDA♥CARE
CENTER FOR
HEALTHCARE VALUE

Targeting Value, Spreading Change

Also by John Toussaint, MD
and Roger A. Gerard, PhD

*On the Mend: Revolutionizing Healthcare
to Save Lives and Transform the Industry*

Potent Medicine:
The Collaborative Cure
for Healthcare

by John Toussaint, MD

with Emily Adams

THEDA♡CARE
CENTER FOR
HEALTHCARE VALUE

Targeting Value, Spreading Change

ISBN 978-0-9848848-0-3
Design by Thomas Skehan
January 2012

ThedaCare Center for Healthcare Value
100 W. Lawrence Street
Appleton, WI 54911 USA
www.createhealthcarevalue.com

To my best friend and life partner, Susan.

– John

Foreword

What have been missing in our national debate on healthcare are practical solutions that have been tested in the real world. In this volume, Dr. John Toussaint advances the wonderful tradition of Wisconsin as a laboratory of ideas by recounting his collaborative work over the past decade to develop practical, value-based solutions in one state. As a doctor, the CEO of an integrated health delivery system, and the initiator of two important collaborations to publicly report health outcomes and change payment systems, John has performed a remarkable range of imaginative and game-changing experiments.

The most exciting aspect of this book is that the biggest gains still lie ahead. Based on what he and his collaborators have learned in Wisconsin, Dr. Toussaint proposes new ideas on how to transform America's entire healthcare system. These ideas are based on three simple principles: Give consumers the information they need to make the best decisions on their healthcare; pay doctors and hospitals for good outcomes (including prevention) rather than doing procedures; redesign care delivery to focus on value for the patient. These principles must be applied together and John explains how to do it in this book.

The most important message in *Potent Medicine* is also the simplest: There is no top-down-from-Washington, one-size-fits-all cure for healthcare. Instead of bickering and political maneuvering on grand programs, everyone with skin in the game—doctors, hospitals, insurers, Medicare, and patients—needs to engage now in a wide range of experiments in every state across our country on the best way to apply these principles in combination.

This will require collaboration between groups that have little experience working constructively with each other. Fortunately, this book shows how we can do this, based on the remarkable collaborations pioneered in Wisconsin among all of the participants in healthcare.

This book provides ideas that can start a thousand journeys across our country to address our healthcare crisis. Through creative collaboration on widespread experiments, we can move steadily from a broken system choking American employers and taxpayers, while failing patients and frustrating providers, to an efficient and safe healthcare system that can be the envy of the world.

Honorable Tommy G. Thompson, former Governor of Wisconsin
and U.S. Secretary of Health and Human Services
Madison, WI
January 2012

Contents

Introduction

Change is bearing down fast on healthcare in the United States—not small change but a full overhaul of the system that will be as disruptive as it is inevitable because we can no longer afford to pay huge bills for substandard care.

As a doctor, a Chief Medical Officer and then CEO of major regional health system, I know that our biggest challenge is the immense waste in our care delivery system that causes poor quality and inflated costs. The magnitude of this opportunity is mind-boggling. The Institute of Healthcare Improvement reports that 30–50% of care delivery is wasteful, meaning that it is of no use to the patient. Translation: $750 billion per year could be saved if we get rid of the waste.

Around the country, various groups have been attacking the issues piecemeal. Several health systems have made great strides toward increasing healthcare quality and reducing medical harm, but are working in isolation and often end up struggling against a system that actually rewards waste and error. Meanwhile, the major proposals for healthcare reform focus on financial structures and money flow, on changing who will be insured, by what rules and by which intermediaries. These proposals do little more than shift around risk and create new layers of guidelines, rules, and laws while the root of the problem—quality—

remains untouched. The largest piece of healthcare reform legislation passed in more than a half-century, the 2010 Affordable Care Act, bears an estimated cost of about $1 trillion over the next 10 years, but does not go far enough. We can improve upon it if employers, providers, patients, and governments work together to ensure better quality, affordable healthcare.

We need a healthcare system that focuses on healing, that encourages innovation without dictating how a patient receives care. This will require a systemic overhaul. Yet we are treating the issue like blind men trying to identify an elephant. Groups like insurance companies, Medicare, hospital systems, political action committees, and think tanks work on healthcare reform in their separate silos, not seeing that patient harm and healthcare payments are pieces of the same issue.

Over the course of three decades in healthcare, I have seen the terrible choices doctors and patients have made in response to broken systems. Necessary treatments were denied or delayed; dubious treatments have been sold. A redesign of the healthcare system is necessary, but it must be inclusive. I do not want to relive the 1990s HMO backlash, or the 1992 Clinton-era fight over reform that failed, or the long summer of angry public meetings in 2010 when people whipped up hysteria over death panels. Each of these fights occurred because people— all potential patients—felt that someone else was controlling their choices regarding life and death. If we ignore this fear, we are doomed to repeat the same errors.

Together, we have arrived at this broken system. It will take all hands working together to create better healthcare without bankruptcy.

For the better part of the past decade, I worked with doctors, hospitals, insurers, employers, and patient groups in Wisconsin to redesign the healthcare system. Working in small and large groups, we scraped away at assumptions and prejudice, asking the big questions about meaningful healthcare. Then we performed experiments to see what was possible and to determine the effects of our actions—hundreds of experiments, done mostly without funding or extra personnel, accomplished by people donating their time in order to find a better way. While advocating evidence-based medicine, we were practicing evidence-based redesign.

In the process, I have come to believe that we must create a healthcare system based on consumer choice, with doctors and hospitals competing for patients based on the quality and cost of their services. Not only that, I believe that creating a competitive, choice-driven system is possible as long as we focus on three essential elements: transparency of treatment quality and cost, paying providers for outcomes, and care designed around the patient instead of the provider.

First, we need to see. In order to build a true picture of any healthcare system, we must identify the data that accurately illustrate reality regarding quality and cost, and then publish that data in a way that people understand. When we achieve this type of transparency, everyone will have the same picture.

Next we must redesign the payment system, which is the tail wagging the healthcare dog in this country. Right now we pay for procedures, so Americans get more procedures and pay more for them than citizens of any other industrialized nation. What we really want to pay for is health and appropriate interventions to achieve ongoing health—a goal that can only be accomplished if we have adequate transparency in the system and can see what we are paying for and how much.

Finally, the true purpose of a meaningful redesign is to reorganize healthcare around the needs of the patient instead of the convenience of insurance companies or doctors. Better care for the patient is the real goal and, with every change, we must ask how it serves patient health. Without a healthier population receiving better care, any redesign is wasted effort.

The individual elements of this proposal are not new. Most of the serious books and articles written about health reform call for transparency as an essential building block of change. Ivy League economists, policy experts, and MD/CEO types like me agree that full disclosure regarding medical outcomes and cost is critical to improvement. When every doctor and hospital publicly reports quality and cost metrics quickly and accurately, the theory goes, we will finally know what we are paying for and can make choices accordingly. This is not a book of theory, however. We have found that transparency is a first step—a rational first step, but only the first step in a journey that must focus on better healthcare for everyone.

This is the story of what we have done and are still doing in Wisconsin toward a more transparent, competitive healthcare system. Since 2003, the members of our independent, multi-stakeholder organizations have been discovering what kind of transparency is possible, how to pay for wellness instead of procedures, and how to shift our focus to better patient care. We have asked hard questions and, while the work is still in progress, we have traveled further along the path to a meaningful redesign, I believe, than any other state.

The centerpiece of this work is a public website[1] that reveals the quality and cost records for hospitals and clinics across the state. If you need a heart valve replaced, this is where you find the comparative costs and quality ratings for hospitals in your area. Most importantly, every single hospital and clinic that has joined our project to provide healthcare transparency in Wisconsin has shown real improvement in patient care.[2]

---

1. http://wchq.org
2. Christina Bielaszka-DuVernay, "Redesigning Acute Care Processes In Wisconsin," *Health Affairs*, Vol. 30, No. 3 (2011): 422–425

This is the result of a simple chain reaction: Providers see how their care stacks up against the competition and then throw resources into improving the lowest numbers. Healthcare is full of competitive people.

How We Got Here

We need a little background to understand how we got to this point because there are still some powerful voices claiming that healthcare does not need fixing. For me, this story begins in the late 1990s as we were just waking up from the long, undocumented dream that the United States had the best medical care in the world. Hospital infections, wrong-site surgeries, and huge jury awards for injured patients were in the news every week. Then the Institute of Medicine published reports in 1999 and 2001 showing that at least 44,000 people —and as many as 98,000—died in hospitals every year because of preventable medical errors. The cost of those errors was estimated at $17 billion to $29 billion per year. And the numbers kept rising. A 2010 study from the Department of Health and Human Services estimated that 15,000 Medicare patients die every month in the United States following preventable medical errors inflicted on them in hospitals. We can argue the methods used in the estimates and shave off or add a few points here or there, but it still looks like the number of deaths due to preventable medical error doubled in a decade during which medical insurance costs grew by double digits.

We spend more per capita on healthcare than any other industrialized country, while ranking 39th for infant mortality and 36th for life expectancy.

Large employer groups used these reports to demand more from health plans and providers. Every year, businesses were spending more to insure their workers and, from the look of the government reports, they were not getting their money's worth. They wanted better results and lower costs.

Their demands were squeezing providers up against another established trend: healthcare was becoming a profitable business venture. The population was aging and there was a lot of talk about the coming healthcare boom. For-profit medicine was the new vogue. Larger companies were using their economic muscle to dominate markets and charge more for procedures. Some nonprofits followed suit, raising prices to fund territory expansions. The competition encouraged hospitals and clinics to throw money into advertising with the idea of branding themselves as the *quality* choice. But there was little hard evidence behind the claims. Organizations such as HealthGrades, Thomson Reuters' 100 Top Hospitals, J.D. Power, and news magazines started ranking hospitals based on quality scores and offered bragging rights to healthcare organizations that were willing to pay.

The metrics that these organizations used to judge healthcare providers were mostly hidden behind a veil, however. Private companies use proprietary methods to perform rankings because they are in the business of selling services. For a fee, these companies will teach an organization how the ratings work and how to improve their scores. The ability to advertise rankings is also for sale. The media are not much better. *U.S. News & World Report* magazine, for instance, states that evaluators judge hospitals on death rates, volume of procedures, nurse-to-patient ratio, and reputation among doctors, among other factors. What they do not reveal is how much weight they place on reputation versus number of in-patient deaths, for instance. The rankings were neither universal nor transparent.

In the end, this plethora of rankings was good for marketing departments but useless to consumers.

It was in this environment, in the 1990s as Chief Medical Officer of ThedaCare, that I was grappling with understanding disparities in quality metrics. ThedaCare is a regional cradle-to-grave, not-for-profit healthcare provider in Wisconsin's Fox Valley, consisting of two major hospitals, plus rural care centers, 20 primary-care clinics, nursing homes, assisted living facilities, inpatient and outpatient psychiatric care, physical therapy, and home health services. In the 1990s, ThedaCare also owned an HMO called Touchpoint.

Like most HMOs, patients in the Touchpoint plan had healthcare coordinated through a primary physician and quality measures were tracked because physician pay was partly dependent on those measures. Doctors were paid for monitoring the blood sugar of diabetic patients, the LDL cholesterol level of heart patients, and for prenatal care for pregnant women, for instance. Experiments had proved that preventive care was less expensive than allowing patients to hit crises. Early on, I noticed that patients in the Touchpoint plan were about 20% more likely to receive preventive monitoring than the general population.

I asked doctors about this disparity between patient groups and they were flabbergasted. Physicians who saw both Touchpoint patients and the general population did not look at a patient's insurance coverage when deciding on treatment or testing, they assured me. I knew these doctors and believed they were not favoring one kind of patient over another. Touchpoint simply had a better process to assure adequate monitoring.

In fact, the National Committee for Quality Assurance, which accredits hospitals and health plans in the United States, recognized Touchpoint in 2000 and 2001 for having best-in-the-nation quality-of-care measures, known as HEDIS[3] scores. We were proud of the distinction. When I

---

3. HEDIS stands for Health Effectiveness Data and Information Sets. It is a set of measures created by the National Committee for Quality Assurance to track care and service in the nation's health plans. It is updated annually.

became CEO of Touchpoint's parent organization, ThedaCare, in 2000, I was determined to spread this achievement to all ThedaCare patients.

If everyone just worked a little harder, a little smarter, it seemed quality treatment and preventive care for all was just around the corner. Some goals, however, were always out of reach. The percentage of cardiac patients not receiving regular cholesterol checks, for instance, or diabetics with uncontrolled blood pressure remained stubbornly high. Why? Physicians were getting regular quality-of-care reports on all of their TouchPoint patients, but not on the remainder of their patient populations. This, I realized, was the secret sauce. Doctors manage what gets measured, and what gets measured gets improved.

A few years after becoming CEO of ThedaCare, I realized we could not achieve the kind of patient-focused care we envisioned without a measurement process that allowed us to compare performance across our own clinics and hospitals, and then everyone in Wisconsin. The health plan's success had lulled us to thinking ThedaCare had high quality when in fact there were many gaps. We were too internally focused. We needed competition and collaboration with other hospitals and clinics. And we needed to ask bigger questions. What is quality healthcare? Is it more than HEDIS scores? How is cost determined? Where do quality and cost intersect, when lives are at stake?

In 2003, I began meeting with the leaders of seven other large health-care organizations in the state, along with large employers and consumer groups, to begin answering these questions. With our own shoestring funding, we formed the Wisconsin Collaborative for Healthcare Quality and launched public reporting of quality data that had previously been hidden from view. Two years later, we formed another group including insurance companies, the Wisconsin Hospitals Association, the state medical society, and representatives of state government in order to capture and publish critical claims data from which we could determine cost of care. This, we named the Wisconsin Health Information Organization. What you are reading is, in part, the story of what we accomplished and how it may affect the rest of the country.

The Value Equation

Early on, stakeholders involved in the Wisconsin project focused on improving healthcare quality. We developed an approach to measuring quality; we talked a lot about quality improvement methods. The more we investigated, however, the more it looked like we were missing a big part of the puzzle: cost. Quality, we found, was inextricably linked with cost—but not in the way that most people think.

There is a common misconception that better quality costs more and that the equation is simple. Better quality = higher cost. In healthcare, the thinking goes, better health outcomes require expensive new technologies, drugs, and treatments. It would be crazy to focus on improving health outcomes with the system so close to bankruptcy.

We rejected this argument. Based on the experiences of several major health systems across the country that had been redesigning their healthcare delivery systems, we knew that higher costs did not signify better quality. The opposite often was true. Higher costs were usually the sign of a poorly designed, inefficient system. Wasted motion, wasted supplies, poor communication, botched procedures, errors that require rework—this is what drives up cost in medicine. And nobody wants to look at it.

As a society, we have spent decades not looking at our medical bills. We do not look past the $20 co-pay, the $500 deductible, or the final hospital invoice so astronomical we could never hope to pay it. It is time now to really look at the bill—at the whole cost of health— because quality and cost are inextricable.

To better understand the relationship of quality and cost in healthcare, and to remain focused on the influence of each, we decided in Wisconsin to focus on healthcare value, described as an equation: quality/cost = value. Or, quality over cost equals value. This equation is central to how we thought about improving healthcare.

To know healthcare value, we have to define and quantify both quality and cost. When we start asking about the value of a healthy, full-term birth, or a hip replacement done correctly the first time, we start to address the full range of issues in healthcare.

To understand value, all of us—doctors, patients, and payers alike—need to commit time and energy to the subject. Doctors, insurers, and employers must dedicate the time to come to common definitions of value. Patients must commit energy to understanding value and researching their options. This means sometimes asking uncomfortable questions, such as: Does current research support this as my best treatment option? How much does this procedure cost compared to the hospital across town? What are my chances of getting a postoperative infection with you, doctor, as opposed to another surgeon in your practice?

Gone are the days when any of us can accept the old doctor-knows-best assumptions. A healthcare system based on value competition means that all of us will become actively involved in our own medical choices—for the short-term goal of our own health, and the long-term goal of a better healthcare system. It is our job, as healthcare providers, to ensure these answers are accessible.

Finally, an important note on localism. After struggling through the big questions on healthcare redesign in Wisconsin, I have become a firm believer in statewide or regional initiatives. While the federal government has a key role to play in creating and enforcing guidelines,

I believe that we must design solutions at the state level, because what we measure has enormous impact on the care we give.

In Wisconsin, we know that if we focus on the causes and treatments for hypertension, for instance, we can move our entire state in a healthier direction. Other regions might need to focus on substance abuse and mental health treatment, or primary care for indigent populations. Hitting hard at the biggest health obstacles in a state will provide relief to the system, allowing hospitals and physicians to focus more resources on improving systems of care for everyone.

More important than local health demographics, however, is the fact that the federal government should not control healthcare data because of its unwieldy size. If the government decides what every doctor and hospital in the United States should report, collects it, and then is solely responsible for publishing the data, we will be stuck with information's lowest common denominator. The most current reports from Medicare reveal data that are five years old and so, no longer relevant. A regional initiative, managed locally, has a much better chance of producing useful, up-to-date results and innovating quickly in response to changing needs and circumstances.

Keeping the focus local will, I believe, keep our attention fixed on what matters most: using changes such as transparency and outcomes-based payment in order to provide better care for our families and communities. We need a seismic shift in our expectations about good medicine, beginning now.

Part I
Data and Transparency

Chapter 1

Kathy's Choice

Kathleen Ceman loved her job. After 15 years spent teaching Wisconsin schoolchildren to speak Spanish, she still called it the best job in the world. But at 63, Kathy's knees hurt when she stood for too long. Especially the right knee. Sometimes, she was immobilized by pain. Just a few months short of her planned retirement, Kathy finally went to see a doctor.

Kathy's family doctor ordered an MRI and said she needed a specialist. Her husband, Joe, remembered that one of the men in his church choir was a knee surgeon, so that is where Kathy made an appointment. From the beginning, it did not go well. The surgeon did not seem interested in Kathy's questions. When Kathy asked for more complete explanations, the doctor spoke only to Joe. Left in the dark, Kathy was nervous about the first procedure—the insertion of a scope to look inside her right knee—and even more so about the planned knee-replacement surgery. She hoped to put off the surgery and finish out the school year, she told the surgeon. He said he would not recommend it. Feeling intimidated, Kathy scheduled the surgery at Appleton Medical Center.

Violently ill from the effects of anesthesia for four days following the surgery, it did not immediately dawn on her that she was constipated and nobody else was following her progress closely enough. "For the surgeon," Kathy said, "I was just a knee." While recuperating in a nursing facility, she suffered a perforated bowel, underwent an emergency surgery that nearly killed her and left Kathy with a colostomy bag and another impending surgery to repair the damage. She never got back to school.

So it makes sense that Kathy tried to ignore it when her left knee started locking up six months after her surgeries. She swore that she would never have another knee replaced. Never. After nearly 18 months of pain, however, Kathy's son-in-law convinced her to talk to a doctor he knew—a surgeon who was part of a new integrated orthopedics care facility at ThedaCare. Kathy liked the doctor and felt that he actually heard her concerns. She received a lot of information on pre- and post-surgical care that she never had before.

But let's face it, at this point Kathy was in nearly the same place she was before her disastrous knee replacement two years earlier: with a family-recommended doctor, acting on hope and faith, with little empirical information. This is a woman who raised a family, earned an education, and had a demanding career. She deserved to be treated like an adult.

What Kathy needed was straightforward information—a few facts so that she could make a critical decision. She needed to know which surgeon and which hospital offered the best care at a price that would not leave her and Joe bankrupt.[4] It is the same disclosure we will all likely need at one point in our lives, for a loved one or for ourselves.

---

4. While Kathy was covered by insurance, she worried that a high-cost procedure would raise her premiums and possibly create a cascade of consequences so many other people have suffered: denial of coverage or rates raised beyond her ability to pay, leaving her to shop for insurance with pre-existing conditions and a history of expensive care.

Full disclosure, or transparency, is a critical issue in healthcare for two reasons. The most obvious reason is patient well-being. People must have all necessary information in order to make life-and-death decisions. The information must be standardized and comparable across providers. Healthcare providers have a duty to give this information to the public. It is not the government's responsibility; it is ours.

Transparency is also critical for medical practitioners. We are not perfect, nor are current therapies or methods of care perfect. It is a fundamental tenet of any improvement system that you cannot improve what you cannot see. We need transparency to see what we are doing and then compare our performance to others.

What is True Transparency?

For Kathy and the rest of us, true transparency means being able to go to one trusted source and compare the *value* of care offered at each hospital or clinic, by every medical provider, the same way we can comparison-shop for a car or a new washer. After all, the definition of value is the same for healthcare as it is for appliances: quality/cost = value. To know the value, we have to define and quantify both quality and cost. Consumers demand—and get—complete information on the individual elements of this equation when choosing other goods. Government agencies, consumer groups, and media outlets are dedicated to collecting and publishing cost and quality data such as gas mileage, reliability, standard features and the like, and then weighing those factors against the cost.

In the realm of healthcare, however, compiling facts has been a frustrating task. Want to start an argument in any hospital, boardroom, or congressional hearing in America? Ask a group of people to define quality in healthcare. Should we measure how closely medical teams follow known standards of care? Or do we focus on how many medical errors and preventable deaths occur?

Quality can be defined a hundred different ways and is usually hidden by a lack of reporting, or well-intentioned but opaque data streams that leave the consumer as uninformed as he was without the data. Health plans usually include both high and low quality—and high and low cost—providers, and patients are left in the dark about which doctors are error-prone or expensive (the two often go hand in hand). Without transparency on quality and cost, the consumer has no way to evaluate doctors, hospitals, or health plans and thus, has no real choice.

True transparency means plain speaking—using words like death and risk and error that cause allergic reactions in both doctors and administrators. A patient evaluating a hospital for impending heart surgery, for instance, needs to see a few simple measures of quality, such as:

- Number of medical errors committed at the hospital yesterday, shown both as a number and as a historical trend line

- Number of surgical infections last month, and as a trend

- Number of people that come in with chest pains and die

- Percentage of people requiring his particular surgery who die in hospital, and how many die within six months

- Average days to full recovery

Notice that these are *outcome measures*, not *process measures*. Current reporting through government agencies such as the Centers for Medicare and Medicaid Services (CMS) focus quality measures on whether hospital personnel complete a series of steps that correspond with the standard of care. These are process measures. For instance, when rating a hospital on surgical quality, CMS collects and presents data on whether patients received appropriate antibiotics, the timing of those antibiotics, method of hair removal at the surgical site, and whether surgeons ordered treatment to prevent blood clots.

For Kathy, looking at a comparison of knee-replacement surgery at 12 area hospitals where the measures were Start Antibiotic, Appropriate Antibiotic, and Stop Antibiotic, half the hospitals were rated "As Expected" and the others lacked sufficient data to report measurements. Incidence of death during the procedure was reported "As Expected" for each hospital or left blank for insufficient data.

"What am I supposed to make of that?" Kathy asked. "I want to know that my surgeon is competent and compassionate, and I want to know his record on patient mobility after six weeks."

In other words, Kathy wants to know outcomes.

A parent with an asthmatic child needs to know how often a doctor or clinic's current asthma patients are hospitalized, which will indicate how effectively patients are treated and monitored to avoid crisis. A truly transparent clinic should also report what percentage of childhood asthma patients can go to school and play sports. An intermediate data point would be the percentage of asthma patients that received a pulmonary function test within the past six months, but that is a measure of what the doctors are doing, not a measure of results, so it is not the goal.

Patients with diabetes need to know how many patients at a particular clinic went blind or had a foot amputated, and how that compares to other clinics in their area.[5] Several intermediate clinical results can be reported, such as how many patients received regular blood glucose tests.

---

5. Doctors and clinics often will argue that this data are misleading, because their patients are "sicker" and therefore more likely to require extreme measures such as amputation, but this data can be statistically corrected for disease severity.

But the average person looking at a bunch of process measures will see the data as a stream of senseless numbers, as Kathy did when looking at surgical process measures a week before her knee replacement. Additionally, a person with a recent cancer diagnosis needs the same information as a person facing heart surgery, plus:

- Expected wait time from abnormal exam to biopsy, to diagnosis, and to treatment

- Five-year survival rate for each cancer type, corrected for stage of cancer at diagnosis

- Cost per episode of care

Considering the sheer number of treatments available for breast and prostate cancer, to name two of the most common cancers, patients also need comparative survival rates for different therapies. Some of this information is available in medical journals, if one knows where to look, has access to the journals, and the time to do that research. Few people have those resources and therefore rely on a neighbor's recommendation or the doctor in the church choir. What we need is one-stop shopping.

Where to Look for Answers

The type of transparency described here does not currently exist. Several states around the nation have groups that are actively working toward public reporting of meaningful data. In Wisconsin, I helped start an independent, nonprofit collaborative in 2003 that continues to work strenuously toward this kind of transparency. The Wisconsin Collaborative for Healthcare Quality, commonly called the Collaborative, offers reports on both process and outcome measures from member hospitals, physician groups, and health plans. It is a voluntary organization, begun by a handful of hospital CEOs and business partners learning together how to define quality and achieve transparency. We will talk more about that in the next chapter.

Several states have begun efforts such as Wisconsin's, and are developing their own agreements as to the definition of quality and how best to publish results. Nonprofit coalitions have launched websites from Minnesota and Massachusetts to California and Washington and those efforts reflect a wide range of maturity, and definitions of transparency.

Many states have been collecting quality and cost information through government agencies, but those data caches are not always available for public consumption. Why? In many cases, nervous doctors and hospital administrators fought hard and lobbied against allowing the state to collect data at all. They worried that their hospitals and practices would suffer in comparison to others, that their populations were "sicker" or more disadvantaged and this would drive down their numbers.[6] They argued that people would not understand the reports. The arguments led to compromise in some states that allowed data collection, but kept it under lock and key.

In fact, there are hundreds of independent organizations collecting medical information and keeping it locked away. Insurance companies have the most complete records of patient treatments, outcomes, and costs, but this data is jealously guarded as corporate property. Insurers use this data to create tiers of medical providers, offering better deals to the most efficient providers. The data becomes each company's competitive advantage.

------

6. In fact, most doctors I meet still do not believe that medical processes such as heart surgery and knee replacements can be measured accurately. Measures, they argue, cannot be adjusted for severity of disease or injury. But in Wisconsin's Health Information Organization (WHIO), we have found a reliable method to adjust for severity. More information on that is in the next chapter.

Medical organizations such as the Society for Thoracic Surgery often have rich veins of data mined for decades on the effectiveness of different therapies, death and recovery rates, but very few people outside the research community have access. (The Wisconsin Collaborative has worked with the Society for Thoracic Surgery to include its data in our website and we are working to include other professional societies, as well.)

Type simple search terms such as "compare hospitals" or "rate doctors" into any Internet search engine and you will get thousands of suggested links. From the federal Department of Health and Human Services,[7] for instance, we can retrieve tables and graphs comparing hospitals based on standardized survey responses from recent patients. Process measures, such as whether all heart patients received appropriate beta-blockers, is available along with three outcome measures: death rates for heart attack patients, death rate for heart failure patients, and death rate for pneumonia cases. The data presented are typically about 12 months old.

This is not good enough.

It is not enough focused information for people facing life-threatening conditions, possibly disfiguring surgeries, or simply the annual choice of which health plan to choose. Without transparency, there is no choice.

What We Found for Kathy

With just days before her second total knee replacement in the fall of 2010, Kathy looked over the available data and tried to make sense of her choices. While she liked and trusted her current orthopedic surgeon, she was prepared to change direction if the facts went against him.

---

7. www.hospitalcompare.hhs.gov

The Wisconsin Collaborative website offered a report on how many days the average knee-replacement patient spent in hospital and how much it cost, although the data was from 2008 and so, a little stale. Kathy could see that Appleton Medical Center offered the fewest number of days in hospital, on average, and the least expensive care. This was good news because, while now covered by Medicare, Kathy also had supplemental insurance and she feared her rates would skyrocket if she had another expensive surgery. As a breast cancer survivor with two knees replaced, she did not think she would be able to change insurance carriers in the future.

From a website run by the Wisconsin Hospitals Association, she could compare hospitals through the Patient Experience of Care Survey. Of the Fox Valley's 14 hospitals, Appleton Medical Center (AMC) unfortunately ranked in the bottom third of patient satisfaction, save for the question of whether patients would recommend AMC. Seventy-three percent of respondents said they "definitely" would. Here, we also learn that AMC scored an 87 on "preventing surgical infection" in 2009. This is one point above the state average, but Kathy was left wondering what they meant by "preventing infection." It is an odd thing to measure, she says. "Why don't they just tell you how many surgical infections they had?"

Finally, from the for-profit, publicly traded healthcare ratings company HealthGrades, we learned that AMC received three stars out of four and performs "as expected"—the middle grade—when measured on major complications resulting from knee replacement. The data behind this score was provided by the Centers for Medicare and Medicaid Services from 2007 through 2009.

"This one was easy to read, with the star ratings," Kathy said. "But I wish they would have given more criteria behind the ratings. It would have been good to know what they considered."

Also on HealthGrades, Kathy looked up her new orthopedic surgeon and was pleased to see that he received very high marks. He received a HealthGrades "five-star" doctor rating, apparently based on four responding patients. More importantly, a single click of the mouse reveals that her doctor has no malpractice suits or sanctions. Her former knee surgeon was not rated.

The fact that Mercy Medical Center in Oshkosh was the most highly rated hospital for knee and hip replacements did not surprise Kathy. Everyone knows, she said, that Mercy is *the place* for knees and hips. She might have made the 30-mile trip, even if it cost extra, except for the fact that she had an acquaintance whose knee was replaced at Mercy and he had a terrible experience. Four surgeries later, he was still having trouble with his knee.

Like the rest of us, Kathy ends up returning to anecdotal information. In the absence of meaningful data, or with some occasionally conflicting data, this is what we have—some facts, a little speculation, a few rumors. On this, we base the most important decisions of our lives.

Imperfection and Competition

I believe we have a duty to report healthcare outcome measures to our patients, to help them make these critical decisions. We must set aside concern for our egos and revenues; we owe this to our patients.

The adversaries of transparency are many, however, and deeply entrenched. Early in our work putting together the Wisconsin Collaborative, the most common refrain we heard was that data could not be released until it was perfect. Even if the data released was five years old and no longer useful, people argued, that was preferable to making mistakes in releasing it too soon.

Let me be clear: The data will never be perfect. We need to accept that, make sure that everyone understands the imperfect nature of data, and move forward. Perfect is the enemy of better.

Finally, I would like to offer the third critical reason that we need transparency in healthcare. Beside the fact that patients need data to make good decisions, hospitals need to compare their true metrics in order to improve. Quality in the free market requires transparency.

Competition is the bedrock of a free market. Without transparency, competition is an illusion. Being the "best" becomes a function of marketing and rumor control. In fact, that is the system we have now. It is not good enough for our patients, our families, and this country.

How do we get to true transparency? Since 2003, we have been trying to answer that question in Wisconsin. We began with less than a dozen people in a room, hashing out definitions for quality, transparency, and trust. It was not always pretty, as you will see, but we have begun to crack open the door and let in the light.

Chapter 2

Cold-Calling
for Change

Every revolution has its battles and I knew they would come. Hospitals and health plans were deeply competitive and distrustful when I began to think about a statewide transparency initiative. Cherry-picking quality data in order to position one's organization as the most innovative, trustworthy, and quality-driven was widespread. We needed a more honest environment. But asking other health systems to join ThedaCare in transparency was requesting a degree of nakedness akin to being out in public in a thin hospital gown, flapping open in the back. We needed trust as well as honesty.

I needed a group of like-minded individuals willing to enter the fray together without competitive worries. Mentally, I divided the state into eight geographic centers, including Green Bay, Madison, Milwaukee, and Appleton, so that we would have no direct competitors in the group. Then, I thought about the chief executive and medical officers I knew, and the ones that had reputations as straight shooters, and picked up the phone.

Jeff Thompson, CEO of Gundersen Lutheran in LaCrosse, was one of my first calls. Jeff is a pediatric physician and, along with his CEO duties, he still pulls on-call shifts in the pediatric intensive care unit.

I knew he had to be *really* interested in the topic to commit any time. He jumped right in.

"There were some outlandish claims being put on billboards that consumers had no way to question," Jeff remembers. "The public deserved better information and those of us trying to deliver better care needed a trusted way to put it out there. Besides, we all saw transparency coming down the line and we did not want to get hit by that bus."

That was true. In response to those Institute of Medicine reports revealing poor healthcare quality in the United States, there was a variety of proposals at the federal level to mandate public reporting of quality metrics. Because we know that measurements drive behavior, we wanted to have a say in what got measured. We thought that if we found viable, useful measures and started reporting them, others might follow our lead. This seemed preferable to following the lead of, say, Minnesota.[8]

After talking to Jeff, I got in touch with Don Logan, an interventional cardiologist and Chief Medical Officer of Dean Health Systems in Madison. Like Jeff and I, Don had been meeting with insurance companies and large employer groups that wanted to know what Dean Health Systems—a large, for-profit physician group with its own insurance plan—was doing to improve quality and lower costs. Don was just as frustrated at his lack of adequate response.

"When people asked us what we were doing to improve patient safety, we just didn't know," Don said. "We had some anecdotal evidence, but nothing of a scientific nature. All of us doctors were using the methods we had been taught, based on methods previously taught. Remarkably little had been done to measure outcomes. We had no data."

---

8. While Minnesota is a perfectly nice place, the code of the upper Midwest rivalry demanded that we get there first.

27

Unbeknownst to me, Don was also in an awkward position. As CMO of a for-profit group of about 500 doctors, he did not have a general fund to tap in order to explore data collecting. Added to that, our experiments might show quality problems at Dean Health. Those doctors would have to spend thousands—or millions—from their own pockets without knowing the results. So, with the limited approval of his CEO, Don joined our group quietly—neither seeking approval from his board nor really explaining to his doctors the nature of this project. Like Jeff and I, he just knew it was the right thing to do.

Still, Don offered a Dean Health Systems office space in Madison for our first meeting. It was a dumpy little office building (Don's words, not mine) that used to be a store. Together with George Kerwin, CEO of Bellin Health Care Systems in Green Bay, Fred Wesbrook, MD, and CEO of the Marshfield Clinic, Bill Petasnick, CEO of Froedtert Health System in Milwaukee, and Rick Lofgren, MD, Chief Medical Officer of Medical College of Wisconsin, we met to hash out what we meant by transparency and quality.

It was not glamorous—traipsing across the state every month to meet in Madison or some featureless hotel conference room in another area. But we agreed that we needed a burning platform to drive improvement in healthcare. Publicly reporting our results would be that platform and we would all jump together. The CEOs brought our chief medical officers and quality improvement staff—our best data trackers—so we could have substantive conversations about what kind of data reporting was practical and useful.

"The first meetings were like the first rounds of a boxing match," Don said. "We were cautious, testing. We were asking: *Can we do this? How should we do this?*"

We agreed to keep the project small and focused on quality. Insurers were not invited to join, despite the fact that they had repositories of administrative claims data that were chock full of valuable information. We needed to establish trust and many of us felt insurers would be overly focused on cost reductions. Since we wanted to report the results of this experiment within 12 months, we also did not invite other healthcare organizations, and possible competitive angst, into the group. In hindsight, this may not have been the best decision.

We agreed that quality metrics reporting could not be used for marketing purposes, and that we would expel any organization that used our reports for advertising purposes.

This was to be an independent, nonprofit collaborative, we agreed, with an emphasis on keeping the group autonomous and privately funded. Data mining is complicated and expensive work, but we agreed to pay for it ourselves, with members kicking in $28,000 to start.

"I lost that argument," Jeff admitted. "I thought we should include politicians on the board, since we didn't have a funding model beyond everybody writing a check. I thought we could get government funds, and I was willing to bet that politicians would not know enough about the topic to try to take over. I got outvoted."

Perhaps most important to the legitimacy and usefulness of this project was another invited guest in those conference rooms: business. Each of the original eight health organizations invited a representative from a local large employer to join, to make sure that we were reporting relevant information. I brought an executive from Appleton Paper, who joined leaders from Chrysler, Schneider Trucking, United Auto Workers, Trane, and a Madison-based collective, The Alliance, that helped employers buy health insurance. The idea was they would help keep us honest—focused on what people wanted, instead of just what doctors wanted.

Question number one for the group: What constitutes quality health-care and how do we track it? Some of us pushed for measuring outcomes. In the case of heart attack patients, we wanted to know death rates following surgery, percentage of heart attack patients readmitted to hospital within six months, and other indicators that would show how well patients were treated. Other doctors argued this was unfair because some patient populations were sicker.

It is true that smoking is more common in some parts of the state, and there are areas where a concoction of Jell-O, whipped cream, and broken candy bars is referred to as a *salad*. While we believed that data could be corrected for higher-risk populations, we did not have acceptable proof at that time. So we agreed to stick with process measures, tracking what hospitals and doctors actually did with each patient.

To get the work moving, we settled on the National Committee for Quality Assurance's (NCQA) HEDIS scores as a starting point. HEDIS scores had been widely used and accepted by health plans and HMOs for years as a device for tracking whether health plans gave patients the accepted standard of care. Heart attack patients, for instance, should get an aspirin at the time of admission and at release, have beta-blockers prescribed and given, and receive smoking cessation counseling, among other therapies. HEDIS tracks this and reports the percentage of patients in a health plan that receives every standard therapy.

HEDIS scores also report how many patients in a health plan receive appropriate childhood immunizations, breast cancer and colorectal cancer screening, the right treatment for asthma, and how many heart patients have adequately controlled blood pressure, among dozens of other measures. If we were to track these scores for entire patient populations, we asked, how should we collect that data, and which measures were truly relevant? At each step along the way, we asked the big employers if the measures were meaningful.

"What I remember is the CEO of Schneider Trucking, early on, saying that the process measures we were proposing to track all looked nice, but what he really wanted to know was how things turned out. How long would it take to recover from a procedure at one hospital compared to another? And if one of his workers got hurt on the job, how long would he have to wait to see a doctor?" Jeff said. "He made sure we tracked access to healthcare."

Then, we asked our quality improvement staff if we could get the information. Because not all of our members used Electronic Medical Records (EMR), this often called for experiments. Dean Health Systems, for instance, did not have an EMR system. So, we tested how long it took Dean Health to gather data on measures such as the elapsed time for a heart attack patient to get clot-busting drugs at St. Mary's in Madison, or how long a patient waited to get an appointment at each clinic.

"We were pulling all of this out by hand, going through tons of paper records," Don said. "We knew EMR was coming. This experience made it very clear how much we needed it and now, we have electronic records in 25 or 30 of our physician sites. It's phenomenal."

Every month we CEOs and improvement officers met to look at what we had, decide if it was useful, and talk about what else we could get. Our quality improvement staff often split into subgroups to figure out ways to collect the same data in each organization, and share collection methods. All of were doing this work on top of our regular duties, and somehow we kept going.

"From the first meeting, I had a lot of suspicion," said Chris Queram, CEO of The Alliance and the closest thing to an insurer in the room. "Healthcare providers were really defensive back then and, in my experience, completely in denial. We would read these reports about how bad patient safety was, and the doctors would always come back with how lucky we were to live in Madison, where the doctors were so good.

"But I watched the founding members of this collaborative have a kind of awakening. They were committed to change."

In the fall of 2003, we were ready. Calling ourselves the Wisconsin Collaborative for Healthcare Quality, we produced a progress report in which we revealed how each founding member fared on issues such as access to doctors, cancer screening, heart attack care, and immunizations. The report was groundbreaking, even though we did not have all the data. Don's group just could not get access-to-doctors data from all those paper records at two dozen Dean Clinic sites, for instance. Reminding ourselves that perfect was the enemy of better, we published what we had. What we had included some triumphs, such as patient survey results for all Collaborative clinics and hospitals—information that Chris Queram's Alliance had been requesting from hospitals for several years, to no avail.

Here is what we discovered: None of us was as good as we thought or as bad as we feared. All of us found areas where we needed to improve. ThedaCare, for instance, found that our "access to doctors" numbers were terrible and we put renewed energy into ensuring that every patient could get a same-day appointment. When it came to educating congestive heart failure patients on healthy living and follow-up care, Theda Clark Medical Center scored 78% while St. Mary's Hospital in Madison was far behind at 26%. When counting days spent in hospital following an uncomplicated birth, we were tightly grouped near the two-day mark. Privately, we all started working on improving our worst scores.

We officially released the report at a press conference in Milwaukee in front of more than 300 people—laying out our good and bad points for the world to see. Don and I both explained our reasons for doing this work: We were hurting people and charging too much money.

"It was a speech that I could have given, but this was coming from two really respected doctors," Chris said. "It was powerful beyond words. The Collaborative took a moral stand. The report was a statement of common values, and I think that's what really impressed people."

The Collaborative's work also ticked off a few people. In attendance that day were dozens of healthcare professionals from around the state, many of whom said they felt cut out of the Collaborative's early work. There were complaints that we were using the report to further our reputations at the expense of other health plans and hospitals. In the next few months, we incorporated the Wisconsin Collaborative for Healthcare Quality as a 501(c)(3) nonprofit and threw open membership to all organizations in the state.

Over the next year, we expanded and refined our definitions of quality metrics, and integrated new members. The Collaborative now includes about 60% of the state's health provider organizations and is working to involve more small medical practices. The Collaborative also built a more robust data mart that receives clinical and administrative data from all member organizations, then validates and organizes the information into reports on the website. Patient information is not included in the records, but all patients are indexed so that we can track care from primary care doctors to specialists to hospitals.

Most important, we set up an information-sharing network so that member organizations could share methods for obtaining better clinical and cost results in some areas, while learning from others how to improve where they had deficits.

This was an exciting time as we built the website, expanded reporting metrics, and included more healthcare companies. But it was also frustrating as we realized how much information we did not have, how much data was just beyond our reach.

It is important here to distinguish between clinical data and administrative claims. Clinical data was what the Collaborative had —details of treatment processes and outcomes gathered by providers, sometimes painstakingly culled from hand-written patient charts. Administrative claims are captured by insurers and reflect every billable interaction between patient and provider. Administrative claims databases are far more robust, containing evidence of every test and doctor visit in precise codes. But administrative claims cannot reveal outcomes. We can discover that blood sugar tests were done in diabetic patients, for instance, but have no idea if the patient was improving. Clinical data does not include cost components; administrative claims can be inexact regarding quality.

Also, administrative claims data has been jealously guarded by insurance companies for decades. Employer groups in the Collaborative were adamant about wanting that information about cost of treatment.

I began a vocal campaign to include insurers in the Collaborative. But the distrust between doctors and insurers was profound. It was clear that bringing insurers into the still-nascent Collaborative was too potentially divisive. Yet, I believed that we needed all stakeholders at the table. And we really needed their data. I went back to cold-calling.

Adding Cost to the Equation

If I thought Wisconsin insurers were anxiously waiting to be included in the Collaborative, I was quickly disabused of that notion. Most of these insurance executives knew me. ThedaCare had recently sold its highly regarded health plan, Touchpoint, and we were working hard to prove—very publicly—that healthcare could cost less even while giving better care. I thought I had earned some credibility. Yet, sharp questions greeted my first phone calls. *Whose idea was this? Why is this important?* On every call to company executives, I described the Collaborative and our work, talked about the mutual benefits of collecting and sharing data, and learned how jealously insurers guarded their data.

Each insurance company uses its data to create quality and cost analyses for healthcare providers. Using this, companies tier the providers— funneling more patients to providers with better quality scores and lower costs, and charging more to companies or patients that used higher-cost providers. Insurers made separate agreements with each provider, offering rates based on the data. These agreements are secret; only in rare cases have insurers made their deals public.[9] The data banks are intellectual property, the source of any competitive advantage insurers might have, and they were loathe to share.

Most insurers knew, however, that they needed more robust data. Each had a limited piece of the total information. For some procedures, they did not have enough data to achieve statistical relevancy and could not make accurate conclusions about provider cost. If they had access to all administrative claims data in the state, the blindfolds would be lifted. It was a powerful draw.

After a lot of talking, Larry Rambo of Humana and Al Jacobs of WEA Trust[10] were the first two to agree to explore the idea of data sharing. Humana was already trying to push consumerism in health-care. The way Larry described it, Humana was still suffering from the

---

9. Humana in Wisconsin now tells employers and patients what it pays providers, publishing the information on its website.
10. The WEA Trust provides health insurance to current and retired public school employees in Wisconsin.

HMO backlash. The company offered managed care in the 1980s and 90s, but people did not like the "managed" part and felt insurers were coming between them and their doctors. Humana dropped the HMO and by 1999, the company's own employee healthcare costs rose 19% in a single year. It was as if people had an unlimited credit card with a $20 co-pay and they were using the healthcare system indiscriminately.

"People spent 15 minutes every year choosing their healthcare plans, even though it represents thousands of dollars. They took more care selecting television sets," Larry said.

Humana developed some of its own transparency tools, pulling statewide admissions and cost data from the Wisconsin Hospitals Association and publishing comparisons. Researching his own family's options, for instance, Larry found that a colonoscopy cost $1,000 more in one clinic over another, using the same doctor. But not enough people were using the admittedly limited information. Like Al Jacobs, Larry became an early proponent of organizing insurers around some kind of common data mart.

We needed a database that included the details of every insurance claim made in the state. This would provide the obvious cost information, as well as some objective quality information. For instance, with an all-claims database we could see doctors cleaning up postsurgical infections, having a second go at heart surgeries and knee replacements, and treating chronically ill patients whose conditions had reached crisis. Cost records tell us about some aspects of quality and that fact made many people nervous. Physicians, in particular, worry about being judged on claims data and argue that it does not paint a complete picture of a doctor's quality record.

Despite the misgivings, insurers and physicians came to the table. In 2005 we finally had the majority of insurers in the state agreeing to talks, along with the Wisconsin Medical Society, the state's Department of Health Secretary representing Medicaid and state employee benefit plans, a large Milwaukee employers' coalition, and other employer groups. By this time, Chris Queram had stepped up to become CEO of the Collaborative and I was free to lead the new all-claims database group. We called it WHIO: the Wisconsin Health Information Organization.

The first year of monthly WHIO meetings in 2005 involved a lot of hard sledding as we worked through issues such as antitrust, data security, patient privacy rights, and data use standards. A big early dispute involved where data would live and who would control it. A data-mart vendor used by some insurers was viewed with suspicion by others. We brought in a trained facilitator to spend all day with us, allowing everyone to give full voice to complaints and misgivings. We worked hard to arrive at decisions by consensus, but by that time we had to vote and we selected our vendor by a single-vote margin.

As insurers were working toward their big, unified data mart, however, some of our doctors were growing restive. Long uneasy about being judged on efficiency by insurance companies, doctors saw the data mart as a threat. Individually, the insurers did not have enough data to make accurate judgments about doctors or clinics. If one company judged a doctor harshly, in a process called economic credentialing, there were other insurers with different rules. The all-claims database was achieving critical mass, however. If all insurers crunched numbers and decided that a doctor did not deserve a contract, he or she could lose everything. Suddenly, it looked as though the insurers would be wielding a very large hammer. Would they wield it fairly?

Larry worked with a subgroup of insurers and doctors from the Collaborative to air the issues and found a deep well of distrust. Insurers were willing to share billed costs, but did not want to reveal *allowed costs*, which would expose their confidential agreements. Some doctors saw transparency coming and just wanted it done right. Others were adamant that administrative claims data should never be released to the public. Ever. Doctors started having private meetings before the WHIO subcommittee meetings to decide their position, and that made insurers suspicious and resentful. Factionalism was breaking out everywhere.

Around this time, near the end of 2006, two doctors on the WHIO board complained that I was pushing too hard and said that I was emotionally involved. In one contentious meeting, a board member raised the motion to replace me as chair. The motion was seconded and there was a long, tense moment before we realized that there were not a sufficient number of board members in attendance that day to make the vote legal. We kept working.

Fielding near-daily phone calls, managing contentious monthly meetings, Larry worked like a dog to pull everyone together, to come to a data use agreement that did not give any group their full agenda, but that everyone could agree on. Larry is modest about his achievements, but I can tell you that five years later, we have had good data sets available for two years and the Wisconsin Medical Society has a program helping doctors understand their numbers and showing them how to improve. The time and effort we put into keeping everyone at the table paid off. Not only do insurers and doctors in WHIO have a better understanding of one another's sensitivities, there is also a level of trust that is astonishing when I think back to how we started. The motion to replace me as WHIO chair was not raised again.

After that first year or two, we had worked through enough hard issues together that we became a remarkably resilient coalition with a common vision to create the first public database of insurance claims information. WHIO is now a 501(c)(3) nonprofit organization. Funding models are still evolving. Ten founding members contributed $3 million collectively to begin our experiments and WHIO has a contract with the state worth $1.65 million to report physician quality by 2011. As of late 2010, independent access to the data was available only to subscribers who pay an annual fee that can be as much as $150,000.

The third iteration of WHIO data, released in April 2010, included claims information on 47% of Wisconsin residents. Version 4, released a little more than six months later, covered 60% of residents. By spring 2011, we expected to release a version of the data that included all state residents, with the exception of Medicare patients. While 40% of patients seen by someone in a physician group are covered by Medicare, we have been unable to access this data and include it with WHIO, due to government restrictions.

The WHIO Health Analytics Exchange produces reports on individual physicians, groups of specialists, and clinics. While the data de-identifies the patients, every patient is indexed and tracked over time and across changes in employers and/or payers. This allows us to measure readmissions, not only to the same hospital but also to all facilities.

While doctors are understandably nervous about outside organizations judging their efficiency and utilization, we believe that WHIO has found a fair method by measuring episodes of care rather than units of service. This gets a little wonky, but it is an important distinction. A unit of service might be a hip replacement. It is an easy thing to describe and pay for, but it does not give us enough information to judge a doctor or hospital's performance. An episode of care, however, is a defined amount of time. That hip replacement, as an episode of care, might last six weeks before and after the surgery, including testing, education, the surgery, any readmissions, and physical therapy. For ongoing treatment such as diabetes, an episode of care might be one year, in which we are measuring blood sugar control along with crises and complications. A sudden trauma such as a broken bone might include the moment of impact, through a cast being applied and removed and rehabilitation.

Comparing providers based solely on unit price is misleading as it is the frequency and mix of services that comprise the true cost of care. Measuring episodes of care keeps attention focused on what is truly important to both patient and physician: treatment of the condition as a whole, as opposed to *á la carte* medicine.

Medicare: Missing in Action

For more than 30 years, Medicare has been barred by court injunction from releasing information about payments to doctors —essentially leaving us blind as to the healthcare costs of 47 million Medicare enrollees. It was the American Medical Association (AMA) that brought the lawsuit in 1979, citing physician-privacy concerns. Courts have upheld the injunction twice since then, saying that physician privacy trumped the public's right to know what was being paid. In 2011, the publisher of the *Wall Street Journal* sued again, saying that the injunction interfered with its right to report on Medicare fraud and abuse. That case is still pending, as of this writing.

New legislation has altered the debate somewhat, as has new information-sharing technology. The Patient Protection and Affordable Care Act of 2009 required that Medicare "collect and aggregate consistent data on quality and resource use measures from information systems used to support health care delivery to implement the public reporting of performance information." It is not yet clear how timely, useful, or expensive this data will be.

Perfection, and Its Lack

Let me be clear: What we have in Wisconsin is not an ideal solution. Splitting our efforts into a provider group and an insurer group is a bit like making Frankenstein's monster in the morning and expecting it to foxtrot by the afternoon. Coordination is a challenge. Funding is always an issue. We have not yet produced the kind of outcome measures that we think are necessary to accurately reflect healthcare outcomes. We need more experiments, from every state and region, and we need to make better efforts to share our results.

Access is also a problem. WHIO reports are so expensive as to be effectively unavailable to individuals. The Collaborative has a free, public website where people can easily view reports on cost and quality for health plans, hospitals, and clinics. The problem is, few people do. At this point, Chris Queram reports, traffic on the website has been predominantly from healthcare organizations, academic institutions, and government agencies. While the Collaborative is committed to informing the public, it has been reluctant to modify the website, given that keeping its current structure is a valuable tool for benchmarking.

To address the needs of the public, the Collaborative has invited WHIO and a number of other stakeholders to collaborate on a new website for consumers—wisconsinhealthreports.org—that is envisioned as one-stop shopping for information about healthcare quality and cost.

Just thinking of what we could have done differently, more efficiently, has led me to come up with a 10-point set of recommendations for states or regions now scrambling to comply with the coming federal laws on transparency of cost and outcome. I have thought through this long and hard and, while these recommendations might not work for every state, it will be a good starting point. The time has come.

Chapter 3

Building
a Collaborative

Building a collaborative is not the easy answer. There are simpler, less time-consuming ways to begin creating transparency in healthcare quality and cost. For instance, you can let politicians or other experts legislate the answer. Or you can work alone, hoping that your organization's solutions align with other people's ideas at the state or national level. We chose an independent, nonprofit collaborative model in order to maintain some control of our destinies, and to shape the coming healthcare redesign in such a way as to benefit patients.

While it requires a real time commitment and hard work, I believe strongly in the independent nonprofit model for redesigning healthcare—and not just for Wisconsin. Some of the reasons for my belief in this model, such as the ability to focus on regional healthcare issues, I have already outlined. But there is another reason that we all know: scalability. In short, the federal government is large and its solutions, unwieldy. State government agencies, working alone, are no better.

A case in point is the State Health Information Exchange Cooperative Agreement Program, which *should* address the issues I raise in this book with the power of the federal purse. Using more than $500 million out of the American Recovery and Reinvestment Act of 2009, the U.S.

Department of Health and Human Services has attempted to create the infrastructure for information sharing across the health systems in every state or region. The intentions of the program are good. With the Health Information Network, all doctors and hospitals would be able to share all patient information—history, prescriptions, allergies, lab results—in real time, across corporate and clinical boundaries. While the government intentions were limited to sharing information on patients, setting up a system to capture and share quality and cost information should be interlocked with this effort, since the data that need to be captured and shared are essentially the same.

In the interest of finding a one-rule-fits-all solution, however, policy-makers have essentially gutted the power of this initiative. Instead of bringing together doctors, employers, insurers, and consumer groups to talk about issues of information sharing and enable everyone to set up logical systems to capture and share relevant data, federal employees wrote a very long, very specific prescription.

In Wisconsin, the state also tried a top-down approach. For about six years, the state office of Patient Office Visit Data spent $6 million trying to create a database, but failed to produce a single report. When the new federal law passed in 2009, cautious state executives responded by hiring consultants—as many states did—to assess the law and Wisconsin's response. The brand-name consultants conducted a series of public meetings and small group sessions, then digested the information and spat out recommendations. Price tag: $2 million. Tangible deliverables: none.

"It took them nine months to produce a report we could have done in two days," said Julie Bartels, CEO of the Wisconsin Health Information Organization. "The sore spot for a lot of us was that the consultants recommended a brand new entity, operating in a silo, separate from the work we had already been doing for years."

Many consultants and public agencies would be happy to study your state or region and prescribe an answer. They may be well intentioned. But there is no substitute for hashing out our own issues, face to face. There are no shortcuts around having arguments with your peers about the shape of the future. There is no buy-in without prior agreement. This is why I advocate the independent, nonprofit collaborative.

If this is the path you choose, I have a few recommendations gleaned from seven years work in Wisconsin. This is an outline of tasks and issues to consider, not a prescription.

Identify Leaders

There are good people waiting to be tapped for leadership roles in your state's efforts to create quality and cost transparency. Look for those who are energetic and a little charismatic, who are committed to the cause and willing to give plenty of time. These are the baseline qualities of a good leader. In a collaborative, there are critical characteristics that need to be present, as well.

Leaders in this effort must be inclusive by nature. Collaboratives need visionaries who are not dogmatic. A good leader must be willing to acquiesce at times, for the good of the group. Good listeners are important. People willing to put some energy into drawing opinions and ideas out of others are vital. Leaders need to make sure that nobody leaves the table angry and undermined.

Include All Stakeholders

The goal of a collaborative is to have all interested parties at the table: providers, insurers, employers, consumers, and state government. Some of these will be easier to corral than others.

Consumers are a case in point. Who can represent a group that includes everybody? You may find consumers anxious to join a collaborative because they are driven by a single issue. It is best to avoid any representative of a group who is emotionally charged or single-issue driven. Instead, look for leaders of broadly focused consumer groups. One member of our Collaborative's board was a lawyer and consumer-organization leader when she joined us, and she has been an excellent addition. Organizations focusing on better healthcare for women and families, or other health-related, nongovernmental organizations are a good place to look for board members. Major foundations focusing on healthcare, such at the Robert Wood Johnson Foundation, can also be a good resource.

Large employers were easier to attract than to retain, we found in Wisconsin. When looking for employers' representatives, we began simply by asking each of the original eight providers to bring a business partner. The employers came to a few meetings and offered their points of view, but many of them dropped out of the effort pretty quickly. Chrysler and Schneider Trucking were notable for sticking with the Collaborative. I would recommend looking for employers that are large consumers of healthcare, stable, and firmly committed to the region. In Washington, for instance, I would lobby hard to get R.E.I, Starbucks, and Amazon.com to join. Then, look for employer collectives that join together to buy health insurance for members, like Madison's The Alliance.

When looking for representatives from state government, start at the top. Invite the governor to join first, and then seek involvement from the Department of Health Services. We were never able to attract a Wisconsin governor to the cause, but I have worked closely with three successive DHS Secretaries, all of whom have been committed to our efforts and an asset to our boards. Remember, a collaborative as we describe here is usually a boon to state officials. Independent, nonprofit collaboratives run by providers and insurers should be able to move more quickly toward healthcare redesign and spend fewer taxpayer dollars getting it done. For instance, many states have laws requiring an administrative claims database and most have tried to keep the work in the statehouse. This tends to be a very inefficient and ineffective operation, however. (Note Wisconsin's $6 million Patient Office Visit Data attempt, for instance.) Collaboratives should be getting private contributions and have a built-in bias for speed and efficiency. Wisconsin is finally getting its administrative claims database, for $1.6 million, by contracting with WHIO.

When bringing all stakeholders to the table, timing can be an important consideration. In Wisconsin, there was too much antagonism between providers and insurers to create a group that included all stakeholders. Some states will need to start with a smaller cross-section of stakeholders and build from there.

When dealing with insurers, be aware that there may be a great deal of tension between for-profit companies and provider-sponsored private health plans. Be sure to sound out the different parties on their willingness to work together, and look for people who can build bridges between distrustful parties. A Larry Rambo, from the last chapter, is an invaluable resource for this work.

Even more than individual bridge builders, however, a group needs to be founded with the stated goal of achieving trust. This means making sure that everyone listens to one another, and everyone offers opinions. But it also means that leaders focus on taking emotion out of the equation and getting to the essential facts. Once everyone agrees on the validity of the facts, trust is easier to achieve.

For instance, when we realized that we needed complete data on the cost of healthcare and launched WHIO in 2005, I was representing providers on the WHIO board. But I also tried to be a facilitator who did not take sides. That meant concentrating on facts instead of emotions. When we arrived at the very contentious issue of choosing a vendor to build our data mart, many of the insurers and providers were deeply suspicious of our number-one choice. This vendor was deeply entrenched with one of the state's largest for-profit insurer. After every meeting, I would get telephone calls for days from various members of the all-claims database group who were deeply opposed to using that company. Everyone wanted to tell me whom we could trust. Instead of being sidetracked with the high emotions, however, we kept returning to the facts. The truth was, several companies around the WHIO table were already using this vendor to help with data analysis and were content with the firewalls that had been constructed around their data.

Peeling back the onion, we discovered that many WHIO members were still mired in negative experiences with that large for-profit insurer that had accumulated over the years. The unconstructive emotions toward the insurer had simply slopped over onto the vendor. There were enough of us trusting the vendor to keep data safe and separate that we were finally able to move on.

Set the Group's Principles and Mission

Creating a mission statement and core principles can seem like corporate make-work. But the inherent diversity of members' intentions in a collaborative makes this essential. Stating a mission and the group's principles will help everyone stay on track, especially during the early (likely) tumult of a collaborative's beginning.

When I started cold-calling in 2002, I talked to other large providers about the healthcare reform that was heading straight at us. As I have said, controlling our destinies was a major driver behind the Collaborative. But our true mission was to improve healthcare quality through transparency of quality and cost data, with an emphasis on public reporting. To outsiders, it may have seemed as though public reporting was the mission of the Collaborative, but that was not the case. Quality improvement was the mission and it continues to drive us. In fact, results from a three-year study at the Medical College of Wisconsin show that providers reporting results through the Collaborative have far better quality outcomes, both as a snapshot and as a trend line. (*The study is included in chapter 4.*)

Balance the Private and Public

One of the first and most important questions that any group will ask is, "How are we going to pay for this?" Collecting, analyzing, and publishing data is not cheap. Grants from a few healthcare-focused foundations may be available and are a great funding avenue. Be prepared, however, to pass the hat within your own group.

No single stakeholder group should be footing the entire bill, as that would give one group undue influence. Even after we had our stake-holders on board and funding sources in place, there were factions seeking to derail our fundamental mission. Do not underestimate the fear of exposure and change that can grip providers and insurers. For this reason, no one group should feel that it owns the process.

Take Time for Consensus

As a man that fielded hundreds of anxious phone calls following Collaborative and WHIO meetings, I cannot emphasize enough the need for consensus. Every time a group or person leaves a meeting feeling left out, grumbling and extracurricular lobbying can ensue. The only way to avoid this is to get the issues aired while everyone is in the room.

Even if the group cannot reach agreement, everyone needs to know the underlying issues and why the majority is leaning in a particular direction. Consensus is not always possible, but it must be the goal in order to avoid fractures and factionalism.

Keep in mind that these goals are huge. We are looking for an upheaval to the old way of doing business, to shake up an entrenched industry. To get to transparency in healthcare, everybody will give up something. We will all lose arguments along the way because, simply put, change of this magnitude cannot happen without some loss.

Set Immediate Goals

Deadlines are a group's best motivator. Set a reasonable goal for publishing data and stick to it. Organize work with the deadline in sight; keep it on everyone's agenda.

Be Flexible without Defeating Goals

Much of the work of a collaborative will involve deciding which metrics to publish. Will you pursue number of infections in a hospital, or track how often a hospital uses the best-known prevention for infection? Whichever you chose, remember that metrics are not the mission. Healthcare quality improvement should be the ultimate goal, with metrics and data publication being the chosen tools.

In Wisconsin, nobody came to the table with a concrete set of metrics to track. Along the way, however, many of us became attached to certain ways of looking at the data. Be prepared to be flexible about choosing metrics without defeating the ultimate goal of the organization. Whatever the group decides to report, remain focused on two key elements: the reporting will be public and will include every organization.

Create Interorganizational Support Avenues

This is the true path to improvement for all organizations. In the beginning, collaborative members will need to share the tools to retrieve data and set up reporting. More technologically advanced groups will need to help beginners set up necessary systems, while remaining open to learning lower-tech approaches.

Once personal and interorganizational networks form, use them to expand knowledge sharing at the clinical level. In Wisconsin, we found that supporting one another at the clinical level happened quickly and naturally. After those first reports came out, doctors were anxious to find out how their competitors were achieving better results in areas such as speed to angioplasty for heart attack patients.

At Appleton Medical Center, for instance, we were proud of our response to heart attacks. If a person came in to the Emergency Room with chest pains, and were then diagnosed as a Code STEMI[11] patient, he or she would most likely receive a life-saving angioplasty procedure within 90 minutes, which was the goal set by the American Medical Association. Overall, 65% of STEMI patients made it to angioplasty in less than 90 minutes and, sometimes, we could get the patient's procedure accomplished in less than an hour. When the Collaborative's first report came out in 2003, however, we saw that Gundersen Lutheran averaged just 82 minutes in the door-to-balloon time measure. At AMC, our average was a dismal 135 minutes.

Cyril Walsh, medical director of the Emergency Department, was sure he knew the cause: intermediaries. Every patient coming in with chest pains would be diagnosed by an ER physician, who then had to call for a cardiology consultation and a verification of the diagnosis before the patient could be moved closer to the angioplasty balloon.

"We are all board certified in emergency medicine and this kind of diagnosis is what we do every day. When we called a Code STEMI, it wasn't like we were wrong 80% of the time. We were right, like, 100% of the time, so the whole system was chaffing," Dr. Walsh said.

Using the improvement methodology based on lean techniques, known in-house as the ThedaCare Improvement System, a cross-

11. STEMI stands for ST segment elevated myocardial infarction.

functional team focused on the door-to-balloon time issue was able to point out the cardiology consultation as nonvalue added for the patient. But the cardiology doctors were unconvinced. So team members reached out to the Collaborative network for help. At Gundersen Lutheran, the cardiology consultation had been eliminated. So, a field trip was arranged. At Gundersen in LaCrosse, the group of cardiologists, nurses, emergency room personnel, and others were able to question the process and learn exactly how Gundersen was achieving those best-in-state numbers.

Since ThedaCare has eliminated the cardiology consultation and created a streamlined process for diagnosing chest pains, the door-to-balloon time in the two main hospitals dropped to an average of 37 minutes. ThedaCare may have arrived there on its own, eventually. But being able to see and question the better process at another hospital moved improvement along much more quickly, allowing more patients a better, safer experience.[12]

Use of Force

From the beginning, I have been opposed to government intervention and laws to make healthcare transparent. I am not always right.

I have come to believe that laws can be useful in assisting collaboratives seeking to bring all clinics and hospitals into the fold. First, we should use every tool available to get full compliance voluntarily. When more than 60% of all healthcare organizations in a state have joined a collaborative and the tools run out, however, a law can be useful in sweeping the final organizations into the fold. One-hundred percent reporting of all quality and cost data for every patient in the state is the goal. The only way to get there is 100% involvement.

---

12. For a more complete description of the Code STEMI project and the lean healthcare transformation of ThedaCare, see *On the Mend: Revolutionizing Healthcare to Save Lives and Transform the Industry*, by John Toussaint, MD, and Roger A. Gerard, PhD, (Lean Enterprise Institute, 2010).

In reality, we are all going to need to use a combination of grants, logistical assistance, and new legislation to get full reporting compliance. Wisconsin is not there yet, either. Now, we are asking employer groups to create a prerequisite that all providers on their plans must report data to the Collaborative, hoping for additional leverage.

I hear the complaints from clinics in my state about this. Administrators say they already have enough paperwork and a frustrating network of reporting duties. People with small practices say it is a resource-constraint issue. Some doctors do not believe that transparency leads to improvement (*for evidence to the contrary, see chapter 4*). After seven years at this battle, I know it will take every tool in the bucket to get everyone involved. I am no longer willing to ignore the power of legislation.

Branch Out

When we have 100% quality and cost reporting on all patients for 50 years, we will have good data. Until then, we need to supplement the data we can get with other sources. Working with the Society for Thoracic Surgery, Wisconsin has been able to get a more complete picture of quality in heart treatment. There are many more resources to be explored.

In this work, we need to keep searching out avenues for more robust data. That means creating partnerships with medical societies. And it means lobbying the federal government to get access to Medicare data in every state. Currently, we cannot see the quality and cost data for about 40% of our patient population because it is held too closely by federal agencies.

Finally, bear in mind that one issue is equally as important as every other raised here: timeliness. If we publish data that are 12 months old, it is far less trustworthy—to patients, providers, and all stakeholders—than fresh information. We need to set this goal firmly into every operational aspect of data collection and reporting from the beginning.

Building a collaborative is work. It is tedious and politically delicate and most people I know would rather be fishing or napping in a hammock somewhere. In the next chapter, you will see why we kept at it in Wisconsin: for our patients and our children, that we might create a better healthcare system than we inherited.

Chapter 4

Impact

When assessing the value of the Collaborative's work, the first and most important question is not what metrics were chosen or which hospital came out looking best. Patient care is our first consideration. Therefore, the burning question was whether patients were getting higher quality of care as a result of Wisconsin's transparency initiatives. If not, our work was obviously heading in the wrong direction.

A blind, randomized trial to test the effects of the Collaborative on patient care was not possible, simply because we could not randomly assign healthcare organizations into groups and have each one follow strict rules. But we needed more than anecdote and belief. Fortunately, Dr. Geoffrey Lamb had become interested in the Collaborative's work and had been thinking about how to test the results.

A professor of internal medicine at the Medical College of Wisconsin and a practicing internist, Dr. Lamb was in a unique position to test the Collaborative's work. In 2004, Dr. Lamb became associate director of the Joint Quality Office, an initiative by the medical college and Froedtert Hospital focused on improving quality in healthcare. Public reporting of medical outcomes, patient safety, and process improvement were already part of his job description. He was as anxious as Collaborative members to know what affect transparency had on patients.

With a grant from the Commonwealth Foundation, Dr. Lamb worked with Maureen Smith, MD, from the University of Wisconsin's Health Policy Institute, and William Weeks, MD, of the Dartmouth Institute to create a two-year study that sought to answer three major questions: Did patient care improve? Did member organizations of the Collaborative change behavior after the release of data? Was there a difference in improvement rates between Collaborative and non-Collaborative healthcare organizations? Dr. Lamb presented his findings to the Society for General Internal Medicine in May 2011.

Patient Care

After viewing detailed reports submitted by Collaborative members covering the years 2003 through 2009, Dr. Lamb concluded that the Collaborative as a whole improved by nearly every measure reported for at least two years. Only the rate of Pap smears[13] did not improve significantly.

Of the 16 Collaborative member organizations that sent data—and half of those organizations drilled down into individual clinic-level performance data—all showed improvement above the level required for statistical significance. For diabetes patients, for instance, kidney function monitoring improved by 17.3% for the aggregate and control of LDL cholesterol was up by nearly 15%. Blood pressure control for hypertension patients improved by 9%.

A study of the slope of improvement showed that Collaborative members who initially ranked lowest in process performance measures shot up until their rankings clustered with other Collaborative members.

---

13. Pap smears are the gynecological tests for cervical cancer.

Changing Behavior

Measurement changes behavior. Collaborative members understood this and every organization had improvement programs of one form or another prior to joining the group in 2003. Dr. Lamb and Dr. Smith wondered how much weight organizations would give to Collaborative measures versus their own, which often corresponded to their own improvement programs.

"In the first couple of years that the Collaborative was meeting, you can see the organizations continue mostly doing their own thing. Over time, Collaborative measures took on more importance, until improving the publicly reported measures became the overwhelming focus of more than half of the responding organizations," Dr. Lamb said.

Of the 17 Collaborative members that answered the 2010 retrospective survey,[14] just two organizations used the publicly reported measures to focus their improvement efforts during the period from 2003 to 2005. Nine members of the Collaborative reported no particular focus to their improvement efforts. Just three years later, in 2008, eight healthcare organizations were centered on Collaborative measures. Six members were using Collaborative measures combined with their own; one member focused on completely separate data to drive improvement; two organizations reported no particular focus.

This finding is an important reminder that what we choose to measure—and publish—will naturally shape the improvement efforts of member organizations.

---

14. The survey was created by the University of Wisconsin.

The Collaborative, Compared

Here is where testing became difficult. Without willing participant organizations to study on equal footing, Dr. Lamb worked with Dr. Weeks of the Dartmouth Institute for Health Policy and Clinical Practice. Dr. Weeks devised a method to compare care of individual patients. Using Medicare data, which included only patients 65 and older, stripped of identifying information, Dr. Lamb compared Wisconsin patients who saw a physician in the Collaborative[15] organization to a random 20% sampling from Wisconsin, Iowa, and South Dakota, and the rest of the United States as an aggregate.

Looking at process performance measures in diabetes care, patients who saw a Collaborative doctor were already more likely to receive Hemoglobin A1c and lipids testing than other patients and those measures improved at a faster rate over time. The one measure of care that did not improve, and where Collaborative members lagged behind South Dakota and Iowa patients, was in ensuring that diabetes sufferers received regular eye exams.

"This should be expected. People who chose to start a collaborative like this were already motivated and were clearly on top," Dr. Lamb said. "Except in the case of eye exams. The Collaborative did not report on eye exams as a performance measure, suggesting that what we report truly does make a difference."

The rate of improvement for all members of the Collaborative, as an aggregate, versus the control group was in a positive direction, but did not meet the level of statistical significance. On an individual basis, Collaborative patients clearly received better care; however, the study does not allow us to conclude that doctors delivered better care because of publicly reporting their results.

---

15. Collaborative members provided addresses for all clinics and physicians in their organizations to allow researchers to identify which patients belonged in the Collaborative group.

Cost

When considering process measures such as whether all diabetes patients receive adequate testing, cost is always part of the discussion. If every patient in a panel suddenly gets blood sugar and cholesterol tests, clinical costs will surely rise, people argue. Dr. Lamb's study showed the fallacy of this argument.

From 2003 to 2007, average medical costs for patients in the U.S. aggregate group rose from $8,000 annually to about $9,500. Patients in the Collaborative started at less than $7,000 annual costs and then rose more slowly than other groups, ending with about $8,000 a year in 2007. Patients in the Collaborative received more health monitoring tests than other groups, without higher charges.

Overall, Dr. Lamb's study showed that Collaborative member organizations out-performed others on most process measures, while charging less. It showed that organizations improved on the measures they reported, and that the lowest performing members of the Collaborative improved quickly. Peer pressure can certainly be useful.

Dr. Lamb's work provides us strong circumstantial evidence that public reporting of quality measures focuses doctors on where they need to improve and improvement does occur. There is more research to be done in proving or disproving the case for a Collaborative-style regional improvement initiative, however. I look forward to more studies, leading us to evidence-based improvement.

Part II
Comprehensive Payment

Chapter 5

The Bill

A man with diabetes and a small ulcerating sore on his lower leg, waiting on a doctor's appointment amid old magazines and the drone of a television set, has this fact to keep him awake: His health plan has little incentive to intervene in a timely, coordinated way to save his leg. Amputation is avoidable, but there is a fair chance he is about to lose that leg.

This is in nobody's best interest. An amputation will cost our patient mobility. Lack of exercise will lead to further deterioration in his health. It will cost a health plan—Medicare, a commercial insurer, or other entity—about $38,000 to amputate his foot and/or lower leg.[16] This is about ten times the amount of a typical diabetic's annual care.

The Centers for Disease Control and Prevention estimates that 8.3% of the population has diabetes—more than 25 million individuals. By 2050, one in three people in this country could be diabetic, the CDC estimates. Each year diabetes is at the root of more than half of all lower-extremity amputations. This is not an academic issue. There is good reason for our patient to be afraid and for the rest of us to feel a little poorer.

16. From the Amputee Coalition of America fact sheet. http://www.amputee-coalition.org/fact_sheets/diabetes_leamp.html

To save this man's leg, evidence shows that he needs more and better-coordinated care. Besides having his blood pressure and hemoglobin A1c checked at each visit, Type II diabetes patients generally need a suite of relatively-inexpensive services that are probably not offered to this patient, such as regular home care visits, foot care, social work visits, expert nutritional advice, and a regular review of medications by a pharmacist—preferably in the patient's home. What passes for pharmacy review in complex cases right now often happens with a single question to a patient's daughter at the pharmacy counter: "Do you have any questions?" It is not enough.

What our patient receives is piecemeal care. If the primary care doctor offers a careful exam, he will catch the ulcerating sore and send him to a vascular surgeon. The surgeon might treat the leg with a balloon angioplasty or perform bypass surgery and save the leg—a less expensive option than amputation—and then send the patient home. Then we wait for the next inevitable complication. If the sore goes unnoticed, or the patient does not get himself to the doctor, amputation is horribly likely.

This is just one example of a systemic failure of our healthcare system, caused in large part by a traditional payment model that has not changed since doctors were paid with chickens or a sack of grain. This fee-for-service model encourages doctors to each care for their own piece of the patient, according to specialty, without treating the whole patient. Every physician works in a kind of silo—adjacent to other doctors treating the same patient, but without complete information on the patient's condition or other treatments. Nobody is managing the patient's total health.

Specialists are not careless or willfully ignorant. Nor are primary care doctors. They are all part of a system, however, that has built walls between physicians, and left nobody empowered to offer complete care. To correct the problem, we must redesign the way we pay for healthcare.

This redesign will not be easy or quick. After all, we work in a firmly entrenched, fee-for-service system and healthcare is a reflection of that system. My former colleague at ThedaCare, a primary care physician named Montgomery Elmer, widely known as Monk, has a good perspective on this issue. As a third-generation family doctor, he has 100 years of medical knowledge passed on as family lore. His grandfather was paid in chickens and cash money, when it was available. Monk and his father both stuck with family medicine, even as specialization was becoming the mark of success.

When Monk started practicing, he adhered to the standard practice. "I had diabetic patients, of course. They knew they had diabetes and they knew where my office was. If they wanted help, they would come see me. If they did not come to the office, there was nothing I could do about it. Everyone understood the financial incentive was disease treatment instead of disease prevention."

Before long, with his schedule filling up, it was clear that Monk had a choice. He could spend 30 minutes counseling a diabetic patient with high blood pressure, trying to balance medications to reality, talking about food and soda pop. Or he could spend five minutes with a patient cutting off a mole, for instance. His pay was the same for each appointment.

"It's not like we are waiting for the foot to get so bad as to need an amputation," Monk said. "We just have these profit centers, these body-parts centers, and doctors are incented to take their own piece and make a profit. The problem is nobody is really held accountable as to the quality and cost of that kind of care.

"Fee for service is capitalism. And don't get me wrong, I am a capitalist. We just haven't been able to work out how to make sure quality is part of the financial equation."

With physicians working in virtual silos—or body-part centers, as Monk said—nobody is coordinating the patient's overall care. Without transparency as to the quality and cost of treatment, patients are rushing in blind. Uncoordinated and blind is not what we need in a health system.

The Cost of Coordination

In the current system, Monk sees a diabetic patient every three or six months, depending on severity. If he had a truly coordinated care model, nurse practitioners, nutritionists, and other professionals would handle some of those appointments and create additional support systems for the patient. Monk's office in Kimberly, WI would likely bear the administrative cost of coordinating that care, while Monk had fewer billable appointments. Monk would take a hit for doing the right thing. Yet the patient would most likely be healthier.

Looking at the larger picture, we see the same issue. Coordination of care means more than just ensuring each patient has all necessary services. It also means coordinating systems around the needs of the patient to eliminate unnecessary waiting. Patients forced to wait for care means that systems are coordinated around the convenience of the practitioners. When care is patient-centered, practitioners organize themselves around the needs of a patient so that a man waiting to leave the hospital does not wait for hours on a physical therapy consultation, or to receive a CAT scan that should have been done the night before.

Coordinating care systems requires that we look carefully at resource utilization. Here, we always find waste. In healthcare, waste is defined as anything that happens to a patient, or any action taken by a medical team member, that does not directly benefit the patient's health or treatment outcome. Extra paperwork, nurses searching for supplies, unnecessary tests, and waiting for a doctor does not benefit the patient.

Therefore, these things are waste. Removing the waste to free up resources cuts cost. We desperately need to cut costs in healthcare, but note that in this model, the first objective is to provide better care for the patient.

At ThedaCare, where teams began transforming the approach to patient care in 2002, we borrowed heavily from the manufacturing world's improvement methods and finally adopted "lean thinking." This method was critical in learning to see waste, remove it, and free up necessary resources. ThedaCare leaders adapted the Toyota Production System's "Seven Wastes" to the healthcare environment and came up with this list:

The 8 Wastes of Lean Healthcare

1. Defect: making errors, correcting errors, inspecting work already done for error

2. Waiting: for test results to be delivered, for a bed, for an appointment, for release paperwork

3. Motion: searching for supplies, fetching drugs from another room, looking for proper forms

4. Transportation: taking patients through miles of corridors, from one test to the next unnecessarily, transferring patients to new rooms or units, carrying trays of tools between rooms

5. Overproduction: excessive diagnostic testing, unnecessary treatment

6. Over processing: a patient being asked the same question three times, unnecessary forms; nurses writing everything in a chart instead of noting exceptions

7. Inventory (too much or too little): overstocked drugs expiring on the shelf, under stocked surgical supplies delaying procedures

8. Talent: failing to listen to employee ideas for improvement, failure to train emergency technicians and doctors in new diagnostic techniques

---

Investigating a path that a patient takes through a hospital—a journey of care—an improvement team of physicians, nurses, and others could see the waste and reconfigure systems to be patient-centric. From the volumes of repetitive paperwork a patient had to fill out at admission, to the missed communication between doctors and nurses on a case, to the time caregivers spent searching for medications and supplies, teams found waste. While reducing errors, waiting, excess motion, transportation, over production, over processing, inventory and wasted talent, teams saved thousands of dollars with every improvement. And then ThedaCare's hospitals saw revenue drop as patients spent less time in our billable care.

Payers such as Medicare and Blue Cross have no framework or model by which to pay ThedaCare for better quality; they only have the old fee-for-service model. Without a new framework, payers are locked into shelling out extra money for correcting botched surgeries, unnecessary days spent in hospital, and treating hospital-acquired infections. Organizations that deliver better care bill less.

In 2007, for instance, a team looking at coordinating care in Labor & Delivery found that a surprising 35% of babies were born "early term" —39 weeks or earlier—in ThedaCare hospitals. A little digging in the data revealed that this high percentage of preterm births was due to labor being induced at a prearranged date. This is a classic example of the system creating defects. The assumption that it was acceptable to deliver one week earlier created a clinical defect. Even at 39 weeks, lungs are not fully developed, not ready for the real world.

While inducing labor has scheduling advantages for physicians and families, early births were a defect that needed elimination. With a new policy and some unconventional tactics—namely, publicizing the names of doctors who were inducing labor earlier than 40 weeks gestation—the practice stopped. As a result, ThedaCare saw the average number of days that the tiniest patients spent in the neonatal ICU drop from 30 to 16. Babies were being born stronger—even the babies that needed a stay in the Intensive Care Unit. As a result, revenue to our neonatal ICU fell by nearly half.

This is the kind of math we do not want hospital administrators to struggle with, but it is the arithmetic created by a strict fee-for-service system.

Global Payment vs. Fee for Service

In the current practitioner-centric healthcare model, we pay for each procedure or individual encounter. The diabetic's practitioners are paid individually for check-ups, blood work and lab results, for vascular surgery, dialysis (should his kidneys fail), and amputation. In this scenario, the patient is a pie and caregivers each take a slice.

Healthcare leaders have recognized for decades that the fee-for-service model was neither cost-effective nor conducive to quality care. In the 1980s, Medicare instituted a precursor of global payment called DRG (diagnosis-related groups) for patients over 65 years old receiving hospital care. The system gave hospitals a single payment for all services related to an episode of inpatient care except physicians fees, which were paid separately. While DRG payments encouraged hospitals to increase efficiency, one large loophole has never been corrected. Physicians must be included in those episode-of-care payments in order to promote collaboration between doctors and hospitals in delivering better, less wasteful care. Without this collaboration to create better efficiency, improvements will rarely be felt by the patient. In addition, rules governing DRG payments are hampering the organizations that are improving efficiency. ThedaCare's redesigned hospital units, called Collaborative Care, have consistently delivered better quality at 25% lower cost, for instance, but receives even lower DRG payments simply because the length of stay for patients dropped below an arbitrary threshold established by Medicare. Those length-of-stay thresholds set by Medicare officials were based on conventional hospital performance and did not take into account the radical redesign of care being employed by organizations implementing lean thinking.

DRG was a half step in the right direction. The next full step in redesigning payments to promote quality, coordinated care are global payment schemes that offer single payments for a suite of services and ongoing care. Here, payers deposit a single fee to a provider for all needed services, with adjusted amounts based on measured performance and patient risk. Payments for ongoing care—annual physicals and the like—would be considered separate from acute care situations.

Let's say a man in good health has a heart attack. He will require angioplasty in this acute-care situation. In a global payment model, he will not be treated and sent home to arrange for his own follow-up care, which we know patients do not always complete. Instead, he would receive care from a heart-health team that receives a lump sum to perform the initial procedure, plus follow-up care, rehabilitation, testing for heart damage and possible complications, nutritional counseling, and other evidence-based care. If the patient is back in the emergency room six months later with another unforeseen heart attack, it will reflect poorly on his heart team's quality ratings. Also, the heart team will not be paid for doing the same work all over again, as it would now; the team gets one fee for treating the initial condition and then maintaining the patient's health.

If treatment for chronic diseases such as diabetes were paid on a similar schedule, the physician in charge of a diabetic's case would find it cost prohibitive to miss an ulcerating sore, or to allow the patient to ignore nutritional counseling and regular A1c testing. The more urgent care a patient requires, the more it would cost his health-care team. The financial incentive would be squarely placed on prevention.

A global payment model would require that doctors with seemingly disparate specialties work together to provide quality care for patients —whether the care is preventive, chronic, or acute—and decide how to divide the income from that patient. Doctors will need to intertwine their financial, administrative, and clinical practices to form comprehensive care practices. More would also be required from patients, who will be expected to follow treatment plans and become responsible for their health.

Determining pay rates and categories for a new global payment system is a very large undertaking. How do we define necessary treatment for illnesses? Who gets paid and over what period? Currently, there are several groups around the country exploring ways to create this change, including the Partnership for Healthcare Payment Reform,[17] the Integrated Healthcare Association in California, the Center for Healthcare Quality and Payment Reform in Pittsburgh, and others, including initiatives within the Centers for Medicare & Medicaid Services. These groups are working toward creating the Accountable Care Organizations that were called for in the 2010 Patient Protection and Affordable Care Act, but that is only one aspect of the work.

What we must do is determine the needs of patients in a wide variety of circumstances and then pay caregivers in such a way as to promote high quality, complete care in every circumstance. Because this work is ongoing, with groups around the country experimenting with methods and definitions, we do not know how global payments should or will work in every scenario. I do, however, trust the process of bringing stakeholders together, with clearly stated missions and deadlines, and then testing experiments. Over the next few chapters, we will be exploring the methods and the ramifications of this work.

---

17. A partnership of the Wisconsin Collaborative for Healthcare Quality and the Wisconsin Healthcare Information Organization.

Limiting Choice

As soon as we talk about limiting therapies to evidence-based medicine, or putting patients into particular treatment paths, we strike a fearful note for many people. Think about a loved one facing a potentially terminal disease, and being told that a saving therapy is not offered by your health plan and so is unavailable. It sounds like HMOs all over again, and I have heard global payments called HMO Lite. For people who whip up hysteria, it is a short reach from talk of limiting therapies to angry town hall meetings and talk of death panels. While aspects of the argument are ridiculous, we should address the similarities between HMO payment mechanisms and the global payment systems we are describing.

As the Chief Medical Officer of a system that included an HMO in the 1990s, I saw the sins and redeeming aspects of the model up close. While HMOs offered better coordination of care, it was never a customer-focused model. A few of us at the top had the power to decide care-delivery models, and we were constantly pushed to make decisions based on financial considerations instead of value (quality/cost) to the patient. We focused on risk instead of value. And to be honest, we did not have a clue about quality in the 1990s. We thought that if a patient was seeing a board-certified doctor, that was good enough to be called quality healthcare. Establishing quality indicators, tracking and publishing that information was not a consideration.

Patients did not have a way to talk about quality, either. They just knew that if they did not like a doctor or the treatment they received, they had no choice. Employers logged many complaints about HMOs from employees. In those boom years, when businesses had to compete for employees, HMO coverage was no longer a benefit that attracted employees and the model fell from favor.

Global payment would support the coordination of care that some HMOs did very well, without limiting patient choice. Unhappy patients would be free to move to a different coordinated care team, taking their healthcare dollars with them. Choices would be limited, because there will necessarily be fewer coordinated care teams than there are individual practitioners. The good news is that coordinated care teams will need to compete for patients. With the quality and cost transparency that we are trying to create in Wisconsin, everyone will know who is actually doing a good job—not just who has a larger marketing budget or more economic muscle.

In the end, everyone will need to give a little. Consolidation in the healthcare field in recent years has left some markets with near monopolies. How to create choice in monopolized markets will be a major question. Also, doctors will give up some independence in order to join coordinated care teams. Patients will need to take on more responsibility for determining where and how they receive care, and advocating for their needs. They will need to shop smart and ask more questions.

I continue to believe that a free market is the best answer for healthcare's future. But we need to know what our choices really are before we can exercise that freedom of choice.

While this chapter was being written, *The Tennessean* newspaper published an article pointing out that obese patients in the state's Medicaid program, TennCare, were not covered to receive nutritional counseling at a cost of about $100 per hour-long session. However, if the patient simply grew large enough, he or she would be eligible for bariatric "lap band" surgery, at a cost of $15,000–$30,000. The news was picked up in the nationally syndicated "News of the Weird" column. This is the natural outcome of a fee-for-service system that is not patient-focused.

Still unconvinced? Let's look at the bill for caring for our diabetic patient for one year (*see below*) versus amputating his foot (*see page 74*).

Bills for Caring for a Diabetic Patient for One Year

Joe the Diabetic

Visit Type	Service for One Year	Charges
Nutritional Counseling	No. 1	$77.00
Nutritional Counseling	No. 2	$77.00
Nutritional Counseling	No. 3	$77.00
Nutritional Counseling	No. 4	$77.00
Nutritional Counseling	No. 5	$77.00
Nutritional Counseling	No. 6	$77.00
Nutritional Counseling	No. 7	$77.00
Nutritional Counseling	No. 8	$77.00
Nutritional Counseling	No. 9	$77.00
Nutritional Counseling	No. 10	$77.00
Nutritional Counseling	No. 11	$77.00
Nutritional Counseling	No. 12	$77.00
Nutritional Counseling	No. 13	$77.00
Nutritional Counseling	No. 14	$77.00
Nutritional Counseling	No. 15	$77.00
Nutritional Counseling	No. 16	$77.00
Nutritional Counseling	No. 17	$77.00
Nutritional Counseling	No. 18	$77.00
Nutritional Counseling	No. 19	$77.00
		Total: $1,463.00

Per Lois E. Kuehl, RN. The diabetes self management teaching charge is $77.00 per 30 minutes. Most insurances will cover it. Some cover it and the person will pay a typical office co pay. For others, it comes out of their deductible. So, if they haven't met their deductible they could end up paying the whole cost. Generally, the visit lasts one hour so the charge would be $154.00 for the hour.

I think it is clear that a patient-centric, global payment system will save money and help ensure better care for more people.

Joe the Diabetic

Visit Type	Service for One Year	Charges
Office Visit	Month A	$116.00
Lipid Panel	Month A	$73.00
Venipuncture	Month A	$28.00
A1c	Month A	$47.00
Parathyroid	Month A	$156.00
Basic Metabolic Panel	Month A	$70.00
Phosphorus inorganic	Month A	$19.00
Hemogram	Month A	$34.00
Microalbumin	Month B	$52.00
Office Visit	Month B	$178.00
Lipid Panel	Month B	$73.00
Creatinine	Month B	$21.00
Venipuncture	Month B	$28.00
Potassium, serum	Month B	$19.00
A1c	Month B	$47.00
PSA	Month B	$99.00
LDL, Direct	Month B	$51.00
Hemogram	Month B	$34.00
Lipid Panel	Month C	$73.00
Venipuncture	Month C	$28.00
SGPT/ALT	Month C	$21.00
Protime	Month C	$18.00
A1c	Month C	$47.00
	Total:	$1,332.00

Month A, Month B, and Month C do not refer to specific calendar dates.

Amputation Bill Example

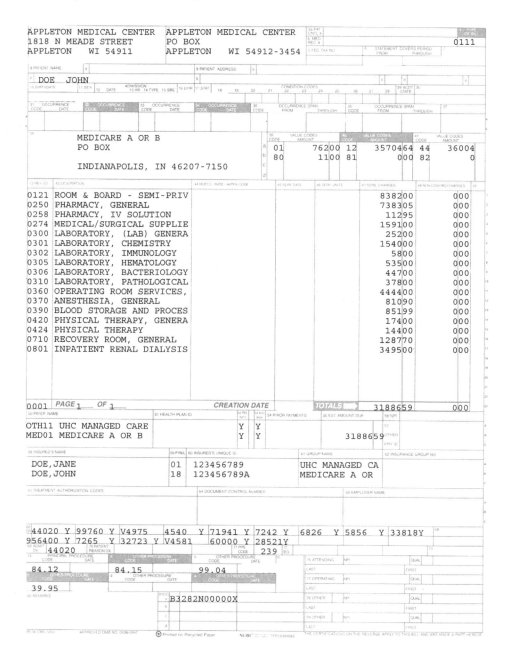

Chapter 6

The Power
of the Purse

Money, as we know, changes behavior. When specialists earn five or ten times the salary of a general practitioner, ambitious medical students with big loans follow the money and the nation loses general practitioners. When money is tight and drug prices bounce up, patients take half—or none—of their medications. If we pay for procedures, we get more procedures.

Therefore, when planning a radical shift in how we apply money to the healthcare environment, we must begin by considering the behaviors we want to produce. This will involve both sides of the medical transaction, as both physicians and patients are affected by money.

On the physician side, quality is the behavior on which to focus. Transparency is the first hurdle here. When everyone knows the quality of a physician or a clinic's outcomes, payment can be scaled to reflect how well providers perform. Quality measures must be evidence-based, and there are standard protocols in use—such as Milliman Guidelines —that can easily be used to benchmark physician performance.[18]

---

18. Many hospitals use Milliman Guidelines as a kind of checklist to aid doctors and nurses in using the best, evidence-based procedures. They include benchmarks for beginning and ending standard, recognized therapies for medical conditions. Pneumonia or congestive heart failure, for instance, have guidelines that include giving certain drugs at specified times, and include expected length of stay in hospital. Milliman Guidelines are updated annually and based upon the latest studies and articles in peer-reviewed journals.

Quality outcomes should not be the only judge of a physician or hospital, however. Improvement should also dictate pay scales. For instance, if Physician Group A is achieving the goal for testing A1c levels for all diabetics, it should receive full pay. If Physician Group B is testing A1c levels on just 40% of all diabetic patients, but has improved by 25% over the last pay period, it should receive pay at nearly the level of Physician Group A. Should either physician group slip in this quality measure, payment should decrease.

Goals for treatment will change year over year as our understanding of disease treatment improves, of course. Consider the rapid improvements in treatment of HIV/AIDS in the 1990s, or emerging evidence regarding long-term cancer management, and we know that quality goals will always be a moving target. Attach pay rates to evidence of quality methods and improvement and the best therapies will spread through the medical community much faster than is now true.

A Simpler Fix?

Setting variable compensation rates based on quality and improvement is complicated. It may drive the right behaviors, but many smart people argue that setting up such a system is a long and arduous task. Perhaps it would be better to set fixed prices on like procedures across the industry.

This idea makes sense from many perspectives. If all healthcare providers are paid the same flat rate, the more efficient providers should flourish. Since price hikes are off the table, the inefficient providers who need to raise revenue will need to confront the waste in their systems. Implementing a fixed-price system could be quick and simple. And because providers cannot compete on price, competition would be based on who provides the better patient experience.

Conceptually, this is the system Medicare officials were aiming for with the implementation of DRG payments in 1984 and additional changes to physician and hospital payments in the 1990s. This strategy, however, created a great deal of regional divisiveness as providers in lower-cost states like Iowa and Wisconsin saw their prices fixed at much lower rates than states with higher initial costs such as Florida and New York. While Medicare officials sought to create a fair payment policy by adjusting for regional differences in price inputs—such as local wages, cost of liability insurance, etc.—the inequity remained through many rule changes and attempts to fix the system.

Loopholes have also persisted. During the first two years of the DRG system, researchers found, providers responded to the new rules by submitting bills for more complicated procedures that carried higher price allowances,[19] did more procedures,[20] and found other ways around the fixed price. By 1986, Medicare was paying 29.5% more in physician fees than it did before the implementation of DRG.

In short, the fixed-price experiment has been run. There is no single price for a medical procedure that is fair in every market. If we try to implement such a system again, every politician worth his or her paycheck will lobby hard for local exceptions to the fixed price. We know from experience that at least some of those lobbying efforts will be successful and "fixed prices" will again be riddled with loopholes.

The Center for Medicare and Medicaid Innovation is, as of this writing, launching several experiments with different payment systems. While experiments are welcome, we should be watching closely to ensure that regional equality is protected.

---

19. Known as "up-coding," this continues to be a common practice—and a persistent complaint among payers—as physicians and their accountants seek the best return on services rendered within an overly complicated payment system.
20. The rate of cataract surgery among Medicare recipients, for instance, jumped by 50% while total knee replacements increased by 38.5%.

Skin in the Game

To keep quality trends moving upward and costs pushing down, patients must also have skin in the game. All of us must become actively involved in our own health, instead of being passive consumers of medicine. Currently, an obese patient is prescribed medications to try to control the complications of excess weight. Blood pressure, kidney disease, heart trouble—all of it can be treated with pills. But the real issue is weight. In a better healthcare system, patients who lose weight, exercise, and do not smoke should pay less for health insurance.

This carrot–and–stick approach becomes more difficult when patients who do not pay for healthcare, such as Medicare recipients, are added to the mix. How can we develop healthy-behavior incentives for these patients when carrots are the only tool? There has been intriguing research on creating better behaviors in Sweden using social interaction and games. In one example, Kevin Richardson—a San Francisco father of three and producer with Nickelodeon's games division—created a "Speed Camera Lottery" that won an open invitation contest sponsored by Volkswagen. The speed camera idea repurposed one of those cameras that snaps drivers speeding and sends a ticket in the mail. Instead, this camera snapped cars traveling at or under the speed limit and entered all those drivers into a lottery. The prize was a piece of the speeding fines paid by too-fast drivers. In a three-day test, researchers found that traffic passing through the well-marked Speed Camera Lottery intersection dropped by seven kilometers an hour. This was considered a great success.[21] Known as "gamification," the theory behind Speed Camera is that fun ideas and positive incentives are much more engaging for people than negatives, such as fines. Gamification is no panacea on its own, of course. There is no easy answer when it comes to changing destructive human behaviors. But there are ideas out there, waiting to be tested.

---

21. "Speed Camera Lottery Wins VW Fun Theory Contest," by Jonathan Schultz, *New York Times*, November 30, 2010.

Patient behaviors have enormous impact on all three conditions in the big trifecta of chronic disease: depression, diabetes, and heart disease. Patients who actively participate in treatment plans to become healthier should enjoy lower rates and co-pays. Those who do not should pay more. This reward system needs to be in place for the system to be successful, and is as important as physician quality rewards.

Since unequal insurance rates can become a shouting point in the national debate, let me be clear: people who get sick should not face healthcare rate hikes. Whether illness is due to genetic factors, age, or bad luck, patients should receive treatment without fear of bankruptcy or big rate hikes, post-illness. Patients with chronic conditions who do not heed clinical advice, however—who skip nutritional counseling, make no effort to exercise, and shun psychological counseling when depressed, even when they are offered treatment—should pay more into the healthcare system because we know from long experience that these patients will cost us more in the end.

Am I describing a nanny state, where we are monitored for compliance and forced to serve broccoli at birthday parties instead of cupcakes? No. We are all free to choose a lifestyle and its repercussions. Patients who live healthy should benefit from their efforts, just as physicians who strive to provide better care should profit.

There are even more thorny issues lurking under the surface here. Many people are trapped in circumstances that negatively affect behavior. Poverty, ignorance, apathy, discrimination, and distance from clinics can all block a person's access to adequate healthcare. These are important issues to tackle, but these are exceptions and are specific to each community. A one-size-fits-all approach will not work. Federal government, top-down solutions are not the answer. The government's role should be to provide resources and guidelines to help communities address their problems individually.

The fact remains that these cases are the exception and should not drive decisions about everyone else's healthcare system. We cannot design a healthcare system around the exceptions, nor can we ignore their need to access healthcare. Reforming the payment system should, however, greatly improve access as physicians focus on how to keep their populations healthy through a wider variety of professionals. This will be true for the underprivileged as well as for the majority.

In the real world, many of these ideas to promote patient/provider responsibility are already being implemented. At ThedaCare, for instance, 10% of every primary care physician's pay is based on quality scores. And every employee has an annual health risk assessment that includes lifestyle information, weight, blood pressure, cholesterol, and blood sugar levels. The closer a score is to 100 on the risk assessment, the better. Every employee who scores 90 or above on the annual exam gets a $600 discount on that year's insurance premium. Improvement is also rewarded. Anyone who is below 90, but increases his or her score over last year's by three points, also receives the $600 discount.

In 2004, leaders at Miller Electric Manufacturing Company in Appleton took this idea a step further. Following a successful on-site flu vaccination program, Miller collaborated with ThedaCare to develop a larger employee health program with the intent to lower insurance costs. First, Miller asked employees to undergo health-risk assessments and, if necessary, follow-up counseling. Eighty percent of employees complied and, within the first year of the partnership, Miller's insurance premiums dropped by 10%.

Next, the company employed a full-time, on-site ThedaCare nurse to treat everything from on-the-job injuries to sore throats. In 2007, Michele Skoglund, RN, reported that she did 2,000 blood pressure checks on Miller's 1,450 employees, which often included follow-up coaching on lifestyle changes to reduce high blood pressure, or referrals to physicians. Later, the company included an on-site physician for about 10 hours a week who, with Skoglund, saw patients individually, managed worker's compensation programs, assessed ergonomics in work stations, offered flu shots, immunizations, and conducted health seminars.

For every dollar that Miller Electric spent on the new health services, Miller's return on investment was $1.48, company officials reported. When they factored in less absenteeism and greater productivity, ROI rose to $2.52 for every dollar. Better yet were the results of employee health-risk assessments. In 2004, 54.3% of employees scored in the good and fair categories. Three years later, population in that category was up to 57.3%.[22]

Other companies go further still, engaging their employees to reduce healthcare costs by using consumer-driven health plans, high-deductibles, and Health Savings Accounts. Serigraph, a custom graphics company with 10 locations worldwide and headquartered in West Bend, WI, has seen encouraging results with this mix of incentives and engagement.

In his book, "The Company That Solved Healthcare," Serigraph chair John Torinus described his company's 2004 switch to a self-insured plan. Instead of a standard $300 deductible and 20% co-insurance, employees were given $780 in a Health Reimbursement Account that rolls over each year, accepted a higher deductible and lower co-insurance. The mid-range is a $1,000 deductible and 30% co-insurance when employees use in-network practitioners. Employees were encouraged to shop for the best prices, with the help of a Human Resources Department that aggressively sought good deals in common procedures —even if those better deals involved a three-hour drive—and cheap or

---

22. With 1,000 people participating in the HRA, this means that about 30 individuals decreased risks to their health and moved up to the "fair" or "good" categories.

free primary-care doctor visits. Employees who used identified "centers of value" for specific procedures got rebates.

In the first year, Serigraph employees on the plan decreased their healthcare utilization by 17% and costs to the company dropped, even during a time where 15% annual healthcare cost increases were common. By 2009, the company was spending $8,631 per family's healthcare, 36% below the national average.

John Torinus and I actually met years ago, as I was just taking over as CEO of ThedaCare. In TEC meetings, which are professional development and support groups for CEOs, we would argue about the high cost of healthcare and the responsibilities of providers versus employers. As the lone healthcare CEO, I was beaten up in some of those meetings. I argued back that it was a two-way street. Employers were getting what they paid for. With little oversight of their costs or engagement with providers, employers were paying whatever they got charged. This is not the way successful CEOs run the rest of the business. John took it to heart.

As Serigraph began a conversion to lean principles, I saw more of John as he came to ThedaCare to see how we were translating lean in a clinical environment. We influenced each other. Serigraph began annual Health Risk Assessments before we did at ThedaCare, and Serigraph became more committed, over the years, to using prevention to lower costs. Serigraph employees are now required to complete free miniphysicals every year, including blood work, and can earn up to two days off per year for having healthy lifestyles. There is a free on-site clinic with a nurse practitioner, dietician, and chiropractor. Health plan members get free primary care visits to a doctor on retainer. And, perhaps controversially, Serigraph offers free elective procedures for employees who opt for medical tourism, taking their business to other states or countries where prescreened hospitals offer procedures at a bundled price.

Companies like Serigraph are putting pressure on the system to offer value healthcare, outside the current structure of brand-name clinics and runaway costs. I wish more companies would do the same.

Making the Transition to Global Payment

This is my confession: I fundamentally do not know how we will transition to global payment structures or what the details of those payments will look like. We will not shake free of fee-for-service overnight. The transformation will most likely require incremental steps, starting with shared savings, moving to bundled payments, and then paying primary care physicians to coordinate care and deliver better health outcomes. These steps should lead to a global payment system that is prospective, paying a monthly fee for care regardless of the services delivered.

No one individual or organization can fix this alone, which is why we need many groups applying their own creative ideas to new experiments and broadcasting the results.

There is, however, some precedent for this payment system. When Medicare introduced diagnosis-related group (DRG) payments to hospitals in the 1980s, hospital executives cried foul, claiming that bundled payments would penalize their organizations financially. But smart organizations reduced the waste in their care-delivery system and Medicare's lump-sum payment for some hospitalizations became the norm. So we know that fee-for-service is not the only possibility.

The 2010 healthcare law is trying to set up such experiments using the mandated Accountable Care Organizations (ACO). It is too early to know the results of these experiments, but considering the profound effect that the federal government has on healthcare, I will be watching the progress of the ACOs closely. My early concern is whether ACOs will be set up in such a way as to ensure that payment is aligned with quality of care or become, simply, a different money-delivery system. We need more than a new way to deliver payment.

In order to make sure that payment systems drive every provider toward better quality, we must keep patients at the center of the equation. In Chapter 10, I will offer a detailed description of the value-stream mapping that ThedaCare uses to keep healthcare focused on the patient's needs and treatment path. For now, let me just say this should be a central tool when devising healthcare structures to support new payment structures.

Value-stream mapping will be critical because, when patient needs are at the center of a remodeled healthcare system, we will also be solving one of the most important issues facing healthcare in a swelling population: access. A doctor's waiting room is now a kind of choke point for healthcare. The waiting room is considered the gateway to care, with many patients seeking time with the only professional with answers—doctors.

When physicians are paid per-patient, per-month, however, they will quickly learn to use an array of professionals to help keep people healthy. Instead of trekking to the office for follow-up appointments, a patient might be best served by a nurse, a dietician, a home visit with a pharmacist, or a social worker. These professionals are not only less costly; their efforts will free the physician to be available for more patients. Teams at ThedaCare and other lean-minded organizations have repeatedly found that physicians are only one piece of the patient-care puzzle. Once doctors are paid to think about the best care, as opposed to the most fully booked waiting room, they will realize that they are not the only—and not always the best—caregiver. Access to treatment will have a broader definition than simple doctor visits.

Redesigning Payment: A Starting Point

During early work sessions on payment redesign in Wisconsin, we split healthcare into three major categories—acute, chronic, and preventive—to help us isolate issues and organize work. I will continue to use these categories here.

Acute care, for instance, often involves a dynamic situation. How do we pay lump sums for gunshot wounds when we have no idea how extensive the damage might be? The injury to U.S. Rep. Gabrielle Giffords from a head wound—involving months of hospitalization and rehabilitation as the country watched, transfixed by an apparent medical miracle—will involve a very different team of specialists than a hunting accident in which a man shoots himself in the knee. As a category, acute care involves all hospitalizations and outpatient surgeries. Joint replacements, organ transplants, and· delivering babies, for instance, all fall under the acute-care category.

The advantage in acute care is that hospitals have the right specialists in place to deal with complex care requirements. The challenge is focus. Instead of applying each specialist to a case as needed, then allowing physicians to treat, move on, and bill separately, hospitals will need to create coordinated care teams that are focused on patient needs.

ThedaCare has created one such group for musculoskeletal care that includes surgeons, sports medicine doctors, imaging, physical therapy, and nursing. The OrthoPlus team is a good example of a care team designed to address all aspects of a patient's needs in a particular event. In this model, a team of caregivers is assigned to each patient, reflecting the treatments a patient will need as he or she progresses through healing. What ThedaCare has not been able to do yet is provide a single, bundled bill for OrthoPlus patients and so continues to create bills from each department or practitioner. This ongoing waste is due to one of many unforeseen consequences: payers still want bills from every individual department. If a patient was registered in the OrthoPlus physical therapy department, but using the Appleton Medical Center outpatient physical therapy center—as most patients do—the AMC outpatient PT center would not be paid unless the patient was officially registered there. For AMC and OrthoPlus to be paid, patients would need to register with AMC anew, every time they used the center, and then register with OrthoPlus again on return. If ThedaCare refused to make patients go through this wasteful exercise, AMC's outpatient PT center would lose $350,000 in revenue. The separate billings continue.

Chronic disease management has thornier issues still, beginning with who might be on the team to care for a patient with diabetes, heart disease, or depression. The issue is complicated by the fact that co-morbidities are common in chronic disease patients, with depression adding to—even being a cause of—the obesity that leads to heart disease and kidney failure.

Next, how will we measure performance? Process measures—reflecting how well a doctor follows the tasks of treatment as defined by current clinical best practices—is a quick fix. There are accepted process measures for many diseases and conditions and we could quickly implement trials.

Outcome measures are more difficult to define, but are necessary in order to ascertain real value. Looking at a physician's or a hospital's outcomes in terms of death, infection, complications, and success ratios would offer people immediate and usable information. Transparency demands clear, relevant information.

And yet, trying to achieve consensus among providers on outcome measures is time consuming and frustrating. Do we measure death rate? Number of hospitalizations? In many ways, we are playing a game that we do not know how to score. Is a free throw worth one point or five?

How will we pay independent doctors on those coordinated care teams, and how will money from a pool be distributed? These are issues that can be resolved, but we need some creative input and testing to know what will work.

Reformers at Work

There are many ways to start remaking healthcare payment structures. In Wisconsin, naturally, we began with a multi-stakeholder collaborative. The WHIO board of directors—serving the collaborative that included insurers—knew we needed to kick off this critical piece of the larger revolution, so we invited 250 interested parties to an April 2010 summit on healthcare payments. About 170 providers, insurers, employers, and state officials accepted and we had a daylong discussion, facilitated by Harold Miller.

Miller, who is executive director of the Center for Healthcare Quality and Payment Reform and adjunct professor of Public Policy and Management at Carnegie Mellon University, led us to split into three separate groups: preventive, chronic, and acute care. We asked for volunteers to populate these working groups and were surprised when 90 attendees signed up. Each group got 30 members, agreed on deadlines, and got to work.

By year's end, each volunteer group designed a pilot project, with initial testing to begin mid-2011. As the work is still in early days, I will only be able to outline the projects and goals, in the hope that others will improve on this work in their own states. In fact, some of our work was helped along at an early stage by work being done in another state, at California's Integrated Healthcare Association. Another multi-stakeholder group supported by private funding and grants, the California IHA supports quality improvement, accountability, and affordability in healthcare. While the IHA does not emphasize transparency in their payment reform work, due to antitrust concerns among major insurers, we shared many of the same goals. IHA working groups had spent the better part of a year defining every element of a knee replacement for a pilot bundled-payment project, for instance. A single bundled payment includes multiple providers in multiple care settings and is given for services delivered during an episode of care related to a medical condition or procedure. Bundled payments are intended to encourage providers to work together to deliver a better overall patient experience. It is a start down the path to a global payment approach.

From presurgical education and preparation through physical therapy and recovery, the IHA group had considered every patient need during a knee replacement and generously shared their work with our acute-care team, which had also selected knee replacements as a pilot. The IHA has four major health plans in California—representing about 20% of commercial insurers in that state—that have agreed to begin accepting the knee-replacement bundle payments in 2011.

The Wisconsin acute-care group began with the IHA knee-replacement bundle and made a few changes. While the IHA decided to adjust pay for severity, the Wisconsin initiative chose not to and simply accepts outlier cases into the mix. Like the IHA, the Wisconsin acute-care team defined a knee replacement as a 90-day episode, with surgery, recovery, and follow-up periods. Providers include radiology, anesthesiology, hospitalists, surgeons, skilled nursing facility, physical therapy, home health, and outpatient pharmacy. The payer gives a lump sum to the bundler—typically a hospital or multispecialty physician group—and the bundler pays each provider. Patients pay deductibles and co-pays to the bundler.

Next, the Wisconsin team drew up sample contracts between providers, and between payer and bundler. Pilot participants were selected and team members created strategies to attract patients.

The initial phase of the project involves proof of concept—simply proving that bundled payment will work to achieve the larger goals. In Phase 2, the teams hope to refine and spread the new payment system to other sites.

"We believe we will prove that bundled payments and transparency improve clinical outcomes," said Dr. Dean Gruner, leader of the Partnership for Healthcare Payment Reform's acute-care group and CEO of ThedaCare.[23] "In a fee-for-service world, if we make a mistake in a knee replacement and the patient comes back with an infection, we get paid again for going in and cleaning it out. If there's a blood clot, we fix it and get paid again. With bundled payments, we get paid once. Every mistake or correction is done on our dime. I have to imagine that every participating organization will be even more focused on correcting procedures to make it right and reliable, every time. Bundling essentially aligns payment with desirable outcomes. That's what we intend to prove."

To test the hypothesis, the Wisconsin partnership's small paid staff will be collecting data on hospital readmissions, complications, infection rates, and patient satisfaction. A report from Phase 1 is expected in 2012.

The chronic-care work group chose diabetes care for its pilot project. The group defined an episode of diabetes care as lasting 12 months—meaning providers accept one bundled payment annually to care for a diabetic patient—as opposed to 90 days for the knee-replacement trial, so this pilot will take at least three years to complete. All patients in

---

23. Dean Gruner became CEO of ThedaCare after I retired from the position in 2008.

this study will be adults between 18 and 65 years old, without complicating factors such as cancer, HIV, pregnancy, or a history of suicide, and covered by commercial insurance. The bundle of services is expected to include regular blood sugar control tests, office visits, medications, and insulin or oral hypoglycemic agents. The chronic-care group also opted to remove outliers from the mix—the 1% or so of patients with the most expensive treatment needs.

While the goal of better healthcare is the same for chronic care as it was for acute, the rollout of the pilot will be a little different. Instead of going straight to global payment, the team opted for an interim, shared-savings model. Shared savings is defined as groups of providers in care coordination teams that voluntarily assume responsibility for the care of a population of patients and share payer savings if they meet quality and cost performance benchmarks. The chronic-care work group has committed to transitioning to global payment model after two years. The team's idea is that shared savings is similar enough to fee for service that implementation would be faster and easier.

In this model, the team will set a projected cost of annual diabetic care and offer providers that amount, less a negotiated percentage. Every participating provider will have outcome targets to meet and must reduce cost of care below the shared savings threshold, and meet or exceed the outcome targets to be eligible for a shared-savings payment. Shared-savings payments will be made up of projected cost of care minus actual cost of care and will be shared between payer (25%) and provider (75%). Provider organizations will be expected to distribute shared-savings payments to individual physicians, to keep incentives aligned.

There is some concern in the chronic-care group that the shared-savings model will frustrate providers who improve quickly and fast reach a point of diminishing returns. How long will doctors be willing to chase procedural improvements when the prize is just pennies? But experimentation is the name of the game here, and the group decided that an easier slide into Phase 1 was worth the risk.

Finally, the preventive care group had an early stumble. After deciding to focus their work on increasing the rate at which people are screened for breast, cervical, and colorectal cancers, team members came up against some tricky math. Getting more people screened early for cancer inevitably costs more money.[24] Even though there is plenty of evidence to show that cancers caught early are less expensive to treat and increase patient longevity, it will be difficult to show payers an immediate return on investment. The bottom line is, more screenings mean increased utilization and additional costs. The preventive team returned to the drawing board to reconsider its pilot project.

Hurdles are inevitable, and those presented to the preventive care working group reminded us to consider the needs of every group. With healthcare itself being big business, we must consider that bottom line. In the following chapters, I will try to address how each party in the healthcare system—patients and providers, as well as the business of healthcare—will be affected by the changes I propose.

---

24. As opposed to getting more diabetics' blood sugar levels tested, for instance, which is inexpensive and helps avoid common, expensive crises.

Chapter 7

The Patient

L ife has a way of making patients of us all at one point or another. Therefore, we should look closely at how proposed changes will affect patients. We need to take this personally. So, let's begin with a common injury and walk through how patients will experience the future-state healthcare system.

Playing a little pick-up basketball, teaching a child to ride a bicycle, or running after a Frisbee with a dog at the park on a sunny Saturday is often the beginning of this story. One sharp turn is all it takes to change a person into a patient. Let's say our patient in this case is a 50-year-old father of three in good health playing with his weekly soccer league. Bob runs to block a kick—a move he's made a thousand times before —and one of the younger players pulls a wild move, wraps a foot around Bob's knee and stumbles. It is unintentional, but that does not change the dull popping noise Bob distinctly hears as he goes down and his anterior cruciate ligament rips in half. One of two crossing ligaments in the knee that help hold the tibia to the femur, the ACL is a workhorse. Put too much stress on the ligament, particularly an older ACL, and it can snap like a stiff rubber band.

Bob will be able to hobble with a little help even though his knee has swollen to the size of that soccer ball. Like more than 80% of the current adult population, Bob has health insurance,[25] so his first move is to call his primary care physician who knows Bob's history, can quickly access his medical records, and perform initial triage. Because this doctor has to compete for Bob's business against other family-practice groups, her office has weekend hours for emergencies with an on-call physician.

After an examination, Bob's doctor prescribes an appropriate anti-inflammatory painkiller, loans him some crutches and they sit down to talk about specialists. In this more-perfect world, there are a few competing care-coordination teams in town offering integrated musculoskeletal—or orthopedic—care. These teams have dedicated expertise and facilities aimed at healing broken bones, replacing joints, treating arthritis and offering all attendant care such as imaging, physical and occupational therapy, and surgery. In one stop, Bob would be able to get all the specialized insight required to receive an accurate diagnosis and then therapy.

Bob's primary doctor should be able to talk intelligently about the choice of care coordination teams, easily retrieving each group's quality scores. Together, they look over outcomes—such as the recovery time for ripped ACL patients with and without arthroscopic surgery—and patient satisfaction scores for the different care teams. Bob's doctor probably recommends a team and, naturally, discloses any financial links her office has to any of the care teams. Bob asks for a comparison of potential treatment costs. Bob is not only worried about paying part of the bill; he has also learned to equate lower cost with greater efficiency. Bob selects a facility and makes an appointment for Monday.

---

25. A 2009 Gallup Poll found that 83.8% of U.S. adults had some form of health insurance. In the future-state, that number should be closer to 100% as reduced costs allow more employers to offer affordable plans.

Around the dinner table that night, Bob's father-in-law recalls a ripped ACL he had around the turn of the century (2002) and how he had to wait two weeks just to see a doctor, who sent him across town on his busted knee to get an MRI, and then made him wait another few days until he got around to reading the scan. He had to wait another three weeks for surgery, and then went to a physical therapist who had never spoken to his doctor. It was typical.

In this future state, everyone has a primary care doctor. Specialists function in care-coordination teams for musculoskeletal care, obstetrics, mental health, etc. The care teams are hired by the patient and his primary care adviser as needed. Bob's insurance pays an annual fee to his primary care doctor, for instance, plus a predetermined lump sum for events such as the birth of a child or a torn ACL.

In the full-blown global payment model, a primary care practice or other provider could receive annual payments for care of an individual patient. Payment could—and should—include calculations based on provider quality and cost performance. In the interim, as a bridge away from fee for service, primary care providers could receive additional payment for coordinating important services such as home pharmacist visits and nutritionist intervention.

Bonuses would be applied when certain health outcomes were achieved across a primary care doctor's population of patients. Because payment information would be public, everybody would know what Group A and Group B charged for common events such as uncompli-cated birth of a child. Employers would steer their people toward the providers with the best value. Bob's family would pay out-of-pocket for any additional care they choose.[26] Instead of struggling with the discounted rate versus the published rate versus the rate charged to

---

26. This is where Health Savings Accounts with low- or no-tax options would be particularly useful.

people who cannot command a reduced price, Bob would pay the same fixed rate as everybody else for care not covered by insurance.

At the musculoskeletal care team appointment on Monday, Bob would expect to receive all the attention he needs for a diagnosis of his knee pain in one stop: imaging, plus surgical and physical therapy consultations. Providers in the care team have learned that having everyone aligned on Bob's course of treatment—including Bob—from the beginning will reduce the group's costs. If surgery is indicated, the orthopedic staff should be ready to answer all of Bob's questions and lay out his complete course of treatment. Because the group sees a lot of cases like Bob's, and the group's providers have worked hard to perfect the process, Bob should leave his appointment on Monday knowing exactly how his recovery is expected to proceed, week by week. The care team knows its livelihood depends on patient satisfaction scores as well as outcomes data, so the focus stays on Bob.

The system works because there is transparency as to the value of healthcare options (quality/cost) and because everyone has skin in the game. Instead of simply billing insurers or employers *whatever*, coordinated-care teams agree to receive lump sums for various conditions and keep any savings achieved in actual treatment. If a group's patient satisfaction drops, or outcomes data starts showing bad results, that information is immediately public and the group loses business. Patients pay for a percentage of care, as they do now, and make informed choices about where to take their business with each healthcare event. And employers will be able to find the best value for their employees using accurate and actionable data.

This system will also improve healthcare and outcomes for patients because the money will change provider behavior. Currently, the system is set up for the benefit and the convenience of doctors and other providers. Physicians set up systems to benefit their schedules and charge whatever they can. Lump-sum payments to a provider team, however, force all doctors required for that care to work together for the patient's benefit. The surgeon cannot schedule surgery to his convenience alone. He must work in sequence with other providers, which means working to the patient's needs. The simple fact of being on a care team shifts the focus from any one provider and turns it to the patient's condition, where it belongs.

Of course, this future-perfect world is not entirely settled.

If Bob decides to receive surgery from one group, but wants physical therapy from a separate practitioner, that should be his choice. It does represent a complication, however. Choice drives expense, which means someone will have to pick up the extra bill. We know from history that curtailing choice entirely leaves people disgruntled. But we must acknowledge the reality that the musculoskeletal coordinated care team will be able to deliver lower-cost physical therapy for Bob than a separate therapist.[27] Do we take a small portion of the orthopedic group's lump sum and let Bob take it to the other physical therapist, telling Bob to make up the balance out of his own pocket? Should that reflect on the orthopedic group's overall patient satisfaction ratings? These are scenarios I would like to see tested as groups around the country begin to experiment with bundled and global payment structures.

In most cases, I believe patients will choose to stick with one coordinated-care team for an entire course of treatment for a simple reason: one team, one bill. People do not like coming out of an often-traumatic event with five bills from five care-givers and questions about who had "in-network" status when. We want our physical therapist closely

---

27. We assume that the coordinated-care team, having accepted lump sums for cases such as Bob's, has worked on reducing costs throughout the value stream of musculoskeletal care. In my experience, when a group accomplishes this it makes care and cost of individual services inextricably linked—and less costly.

aligned with surgeons and nurses. We want straight answers about costs —not a complicated spreadsheet showing costs, discount pricing, and details about every aspirin given. Those complicated bills represent waste for providers, as well. Less accounting will be a bonus for everyone. Still, patients should have the choice to fragment care if they wish.

Keeping medical costs low in less-populated areas will also be a challenge. Competition drives down cost and creates better value (as long as there is transparency of quality outcomes, of course). But rural areas will be a challenge. The growing popularity of web-based teleconferencing may provide part of the answer, with city-based coordinated-care teams offering splinter clinics in rural areas, supplemented by doctors consulting at a distance.

What of those physicians, though? Pushed out of their independent offices to join teams of other providers, losing status as the center of the medical solar system—what does this new world hold for doctors?

Chapter 8

Physicians' Future

Nathan Grunwald is the future of medicine and he is worried. A primary care physician in ThedaCare's Menasha Clinic just five years out of residency, Dr. Grunwald is also a pretty modest guy and would probably want me to point out that he is just one piece of the future of medicine. He is worried for good cause, though, since healthcare's center of gravity is shifting to the family doctor and there are too few to go around.

During medical school in Milwaukee, people would tell him that he was a smart person—too smart for family medicine. He could go into any of the specialties, they said, and make a lot more money. Nearly all of Grunwald's professors were specialists—as is true in medical schools around the country—and each talked up the importance of his or her field.

Grunwald loved those six-week rotations through cardiology, orthopedics, gastroenterology, pediatrics, and OB/GYN. Finding that he enjoyed all the specialties confirmed his decision to go home to Neenah and be a family doctor. But he still finds himself defending his decision sometimes.

"I love my job because, when a mother comes in with a fussy child, I can diagnose and treat the child's earaches, and then help that mother with her sleeplessness, and maybe take a look at her husband's rash and treat that, too. Who has time to go running around to all those specialists?" Dr. Grunwald said. "This is so much more cost-effective."

To offer quality healthcare to all—including an estimated 30 million Americans who are currently uninsured—we need family practitioners like Dr. Grunwald. Primary care doctors intervene early to keep minor maladies from becoming life-threatening. They catch and relieve childhood asthma, tell us when we are putting on too much weight or when our blood sugars are out of whack, track our vaccines, flu shots, and cancer screenings. Half the babies born in Wisconsin do so with the help of a family doctor. Dr. Grunwald knows the critical position he occupies and he is caught between his vision of quality and an increasingly dire sense of necessity.

"I would love to spend an hour with each patient, to make sure they are getting really top-notch care. But there aren't enough of us. People are being left out if I'm spending all the time I want with each patient. Patients are not getting care if they aren't being seen," Dr. Grunwald said. "I'm nervous about how we will meet patient needs in the future."

The Association of American Medical Colleges estimated that the country needed another 9,000 primary care physicians to meet medical needs in 2010. In 2025, we will be short by 65,800.[28] Yet, the number of medical students entering family medicine fell more than 25% between 2002 and 2007.[29] Incentives to encourage more students into family medicine have been debated and considered. But the proposal that made it into the final version of the 2010 Affordable Care Act, offering a 10% Medicare pay boost for primary care doctors,

---

28. https://www.aamc.org/download/158076/data/updated_projections_through_2025.pdf
29. "Medical Schools Can't Keep Up," Suzanne Sataline and Shirley S. Wang, *Wall Street Journal*, April 12, 2010.

does not go far enough. We cannot simply hope that ambitious young medical students will choose family medicine for the greater good. Every serious version of healthcare redesign, after all, places new emphasis on these front-line physicians.

Family doctors—especially the solo-practitioner variety—will find their businesses changing even while they are in greater demand. The move away from the country-doctor model has been happening for years, with just 18% of members of the American Academy of Family Physicians being solo practitioners in 2008, down from 44% in 1986. In a global payment system, primary care doctors will need to be team leaders instead of small business owners. They might be part of a large healthcare system, or have an office with fellow primary care doctors, nurse practitioners, and strong ties to a number of health organizations. In either case, however, primary care doctors will coordinate all the professionals needed to keep their patients healthy, such as nurses, social workers, pharmacists, nutritionists, lab technicians, and even specialists. The family-practice clinics that provide the best, most comprehensive healthcare and help patients stay well will get the most contracts. Those that work to remove waste from their processes while improving their patient-focused care will make the most money.

Hear that outcry? Those are doctors complaining that their patients are sicker, fatter, or more stressed by environmental factors, and so their financial risk is greater in a global payment system. How can they make money when their patients need more care than others need?

First, let's remember that extensive studies at Dartmouth University have shown that there is no correlation between population health and healthcare costs. Cities and regions with the highest per-capita healthcare costs simply do not have sicker people, nor do they have better healthcare.[30]

---

30. The Dartmouth Atlas of Health Care, for instance, shows that McAllen, TX, has the highest rate of Medicare reimbursements in the nation, yet one of the lowest national percentages of Medicare enrollees that are receiving appropriate diabetes care. See: www.dartmouthatlas.org

Then, we need to acknowledge that risk is going to be a thorny issue for doctors. We will discuss risk more thoroughly in the next chapter, but let's look at the most pervasive threat to a doctor's finances. In this system, Dr. Grunwald would have a consistent number of patients. Perhaps he would be responsible for 2,500 lives and be paid a set annual amount for each person, adjusted for the person's previous health. Of those 2,500 lives, about 50% suffer from chronic conditions such as diabetes, congestive heart failure, and depression.[31] Dr. Grunwald's job is to help his chronic patients control their disease and work on improving the underlying causes.

In any group of chronic patients, 10–15% typically have uncontrolled symptoms of disease. Most of these patients are noncompliant—they are not changing their diets, getting more exercise, or participating fully in treatment plans. The cost of caring for these patients can suddenly skyrocket as emergencies arise, placing great strain on a clinic. In all, a practice might include 125 patients who are at risk for expensive emergencies at any time. This scenario would keep Dr. Grunwald up at night, if he were self-employed.

There are remedies under investigation, however. In 2008, a business coalition with 100,000 members approached ThedaCare asking for help in developing a new model for caring for noncompliant chronic disease sufferers. Using value-stream analysis and a multi-stakeholder approach, a team focused on coronary disease—accounting for $93 million a year in the coalition's health costs—and came up with the idea of an Ambulatory Intensive Care Unit.

Essentially, the Ambulatory ICU is a way to remove the highest-risk patients from a doctor's patient panel while getting sick people the care they need. Think of it as boot camp for people with uncontrolled

---

31. In a 2009 report, the Centers for Disease Control estimated that 133 million Americans —a little more than one in three people—live with one or more chronic illnesses. One quarter of those affected experience significant limitations in their daily activities. http://www.cdc.gov/chronicdisease/resources/publications/AAG/chronic.htm

disease. Those who joined would agree to work with the Ambulatory ICU's care-coordination team, including pharmacists, behavioral health and public health workers, nurses, dieticians, and other professionals. Patients might meet with a pharmacist monthly and a dietician weekly, learning how to embrace behaviors and daily decisions that would lead to better health. Individualized plans and frequent lab work would remove the guesswork from treatment.

Treating 10,000 patients with coronary disease in an Ambulatory ICU would cost about $1 million a year, the team estimated. Total savings achieved by bringing those patients' symptoms into control: $20 million annually.[32]

The Ambulatory ICU, however, remains no more than an intriguing theory. The coalition's CEOs were unwilling to take on $1 million in annual costs for a projected annual savings of $20 million. To be fair, the proposal was delivered to the CEOs in 2008, during the worst financial meltdown the country had seen since 1929. Still, it is discouraging that we cannot report results from a trial run.

Show Me the Money

Without a trace of irony, Dr. Grunwald says, "Some of my best friends are specialists." The only problem with his friends? They make a lot more money than he does. An orthopedic surgeon, for instance, can fix the torn ligament of a 23-year-old swimmer in an afternoon, Grunwald said, and make multiples of what he does caring for a diabetic for her entire life.

"I do think there needs to be a leveling of compensation," said Dr. Grunwald.

---

32. See the complete case study for an Ambulatory ICU at
    www.createhealthcarevalue.com/resources/case-studies/ambulatory_icu/

Hear that roar of opposition? That is the sound of about 600,000 specialists claiming that primary care doctors will use this opportunity to grab a larger slice of a shrinking pie.

Welcome to the cage match that is compensation negotiations among physicians. Beginning in the late 1990s when I was Chief Medical Officer of ThedaCare, the parent company of the HMO, Touchpoint, I witnessed firsthand the distrust of physicians who need to share from the same pot of money. I saw anesthesiologists dig in, claiming that surgeries cannot happen without their expertise and so they deserved more money. Surgeons claimed their skills and extra training warranted a lot more money than primary care doctors. And I saw primary care physicians retaliate by refusing to refer their patients to the most outspoken of those surgeons.

I do believe that compensation for primary care physicians needs to be aligned with the pivotal role they will occupy in the new system. Current incentives urge students into specialty medicine. But the only way we are going to afford healthcare for all is to fundamentally change the system to emphasize prevention over late-stage, expensive procedures. That means paying primary care physicians more and recognizing there will be little incentive, in a global payment model, to do expensive procedures. Hence, we will need fewer specialists.

None of this goes down well with my old friend Jeffrey Whiteside. An independent pulmonologist in an office of five other lung specialists, Dr. Whiteside has nearly 30 years' experience with the sickest patients in Wisconsin's Fox Valley. He and his partners run the Intensive Care Units at two hospitals, overseeing 26 beds, where he cares for the sickest of the sick—those attached to ventilators, often in the last days or weeks of life. In his office, he sees outpatients suffering from emphysema, asthma, lung cancer, and sleep apnea. Dr. Whiteside thinks the current fee-for-service can and does work, although it might need a few modifications. More than that, he is deeply suspicious of not being paid per patient.

"We work nights and weekends," Dr. Whiteside said of independent physicians like himself. "What would motivate us to get up at 3 a.m. and go out into a snowstorm for someone in the ICU, except knowing that we have to do a good job on every person or we starve?

"Look, we can sing *kumbaya* and believe everybody in a system will do a good job, but we know some people won't pull their weight if they don't have to."

Dr. Whiteside believes that a steady paycheck from a care-coordination team could demotivate physicians. He does not believe that the quality of a doctor's work can be captured in outcomes data—at least, he has not yet seen it done accurately, he says—and he is worried that independent specialists will lose in this new system. Independent specialists like Dr. Whiteside and his partners would have to negotiate fees with 50 different primary care physicians, he said, and he does not picture coming out a winner there.

But here is Dr. Whiteside's greatest concern: healthcare systems like the one being proposed here focus on saving money by doing fewer tests and fewer procedures, he said. In short, he says, money will be saved by giving patients less.

"I realize that someone has to step forward and say we can't pay for all this stuff anymore. I know that 25% of a person's lifetime medical dollars are spent in the last two weeks of life," Dr. Whiteside said. "But you know what matters to an 80-year-old with lung disease? Living."

Touching the Third Rail of Healthcare Politics

End-of-life care is the specter in the room of every healthcare debate. This is where the high cost of heroic measures for a dying person run smack into a collective will to live and often, a profound fear of death. Anyone trying to discuss a reduction in end-of-life care is hit with accusations of running a death panel—deciding who is worth the cost of life-extending measures and who is not.

It is time to have grown-up conversations about the end of life. In doing so, we can expand the debate about the care we want to receive throughout our lives.

It has been well documented that when patients have complete information on all possible options, a majority will chose the least invasive, least complicated, least expensive procedure. If a doctor says, "You need surgery," people will have surgery. But if all options are presented, including physical therapy and less-invasive drug therapies, people tend to choose the latter.

Consider the case of lung volume reduction surgery. In the 1990s, this very expensive operation that involves cutting away diseased sections of lung in order to give healthy tissue room to expand was gaining in popularity. Surgeons were billing Medicare for the procedure under existing codes and offering testimonials on the "miracle" surgery for emphysema patients. Facing the potential of thousands of these surgeries a year, costing about $50,000 each including rehabilitation, Medicare was looking at a budget buster.

Unable by law to consider cost when approving specific treatments, Medicare officials instead sponsored a clinical trial of the surgery with the National Heart, Lung and Blood Institute. Published in 2003 following a four-year trial, results showed that patients in the study generally lived no longer whether they had the surgery or not. There were some variations in the numbers, and some patients with a specific type of condition found it easier to walk or breathe. But the numbers made it clear that the surgery was no panacea.

Medicare officials released the study, approved the surgery, and braced themselves for the bill. It did not come. When doctors discussed the surgery and clinical trial with patients, demand for lung volume reduction surgery—previously driven by anecdote and testimonial —dried up.

"It's difficult to sign someone up for a 50-thousand-dollar-plus operation with an 8% upfront mortality risk," Dr. Mark Dransfield, a pulmonologist at the University of Alabama at Birmingham told the *New York Times*' Gina Kolata in an 2006 article about response to the clinical trial. Dr. David Mannino, a pulmonologist at the University of Kentucky, added that after he began presenting his patients with the Medicare study, they invariably declined the operation.

"We talk about risks and benefits and they say, 'Let me try pulmonary rehabilitation instead,' " Dr. Mannino told Kolata.[33]

In general, specialists drive more procedures, more chemotherapy, and new surgical techniques. That is how they are paid. Their focus is to kill cancer cells and cut out diseased tissue, not necessarily to consider the patient's quality of life. The goal for too long has been to extend life, without enough consideration as to the quality of that life.

In the past 20 years, Dr. Whiteside reports, there has been a lot more talk about advance directives. Medicare rules state that he must ask his very sick patients about do-not-resuscitate orders and end-of-life decisions—"Another 20-minute conversation I don't get paid for,"

---

33. "Medicare Says it Will Pay, But Patients Say 'No Thanks'," Gina Kolata, *The New York Times*, March 3, 2006

he points out—and has found that people are more realistic. Dr. Whiteside may still need to have long discussions with a frail 98-year-old woman as to why he will not operate on her lungs, but finds that people are generally reasonable.

"There are just a lot more elderly people and more are coming," he said. "And people are still breaking down the door to see me."

Doctors Grunwald and Whiteside are not very different. They both care deeply about their patients and want to offer the best care. They each look ahead to the coming changes with some trepidation—realizing the system must change in order to avoid bankruptcy, and worried about what it will mean for them and their patients. The disparities in their concerns give us some insight into the debates ahead.

Physicians, however, are not the sum total of the healthcare system, nor will they be the loudest voices. Business interests in healthcare have out-sized influence to drive legislation and shape the debate. So we need to look closely at how global payments might change the business side.

Chapter 9

The Business End

As the former CEO of a healthcare organization, I know too well the stress that this redesign is placing on the business of medicine. Already slammed with daily emergencies, healthcare leaders now must prepare for a future of rapidly shifting landscapes, in which both risk and reward are moving targets.

The 2010 Affordable Care Act and the proposals I put forward here mean that most CEOs will need to exit their silos. In a more integrated system, leaders must join with other organizations to provide comprehensive service to patients. The problem is that current laws interfere with collaborations across boundaries. Getting providers working together will require a reexamination of antitrust rules and Stark Laws.[34] Healthcare business leaders need politicians to get involved now and begin realigning laws to work for the future of healthcare.

While the Affordable Care Act of 2010 recognized the need for collaboration and called for physicians to join in Accountable Care Organizations, it was not clear as of this writing that ACOs would

---

34. Named for U.S. Rep. Pete Stark of California, these laws prohibit doctors from referring patients to treatment centers in which the doctor has a financial interest. The laws are complex and filled with exceptions, but the main complaint with Stark II, as written, is that it discourages physicians from joining managed care groups.

actually facilitate integrated care. It is not enough for doctors to bill together. We need a collaborative model that focuses everyone's energies on unified patient care. That requires breaking down silos to encourage both financial and clinical integration. When independent physicians become part of a larger treatment plan instead of body-part specialists operating in silos, patient care becomes less fragmented. That is the reward for everyone. The risk part of this equation is the sticking point.

Simply put, hospitals, health systems, and coordinated-care groups large and small will now bear the financial risk of catastrophic illness befalling patients. In the current system, employers and insurers bear that risk. If a business had 100 employees and there was a heart attack, a stage-three cancer and a bad car accident all in the same year, insurance rates rose astronomically. Businesses sometimes went bankrupt after such years. The ones that survived often joined alliances to form healthcare buying groups to spread the risk—a good tactic that helped everyone delay confronting the ultimate truth: Healthcare prices were simply too high.

In a global payment system, where physician groups and health plans agree to a single per-member, per-month payment for all services delivered to a patient, with payment adjustments based on measured performance and patient risk, providers assume the financial risk. This means regional and mid-sized healthcare providers that form the bedrock of competition in most places are now in the position of any small business. A natural disaster, a cancer cluster, a couple of bad years could wipe them out.

The immediate response to this impending risk among healthcare executives has been a rush to consolidate. Beginning in the 1990s, medicine started to shift from a collection of independent physicians and nonprofit community hospitals to larger, brand-name corporations.

This trend has picked up steam as major healthcare reform went from rumor to certainty. As large corporate providers prepared to assume risk, they swallowed smaller providers and began dominating regional markets. Johns Hopkins Medicine, for instance—with a major hospital and 25 clinics in Maryland—bought Sibley Memorial Hospital in Washington less than two years after buying Suburban Hospital in Bethesda. In Wisconsin, ThedaCare merged with Shawano Medical Center in the fall of 2010, but still is not even a quarter the size of Aurora Health Care. This dominant player in eastern Wisconsin has been expanding rapidly in the past 20 years, adding about two dozen hospitals and clinics to its roster through mergers or site building.[35]

The reason large healthcare companies are growing larger is that leaders hope to dominate regions and control pricing. By "control pricing," of course, I mean, "charge whatever they want." We know that healthcare prices rise where monopolies exist, so this rapid consolidation is a dangerous trend. This current upheaval of the health-care system became a certainty, after all, because the high cost of care was bankrupting families, businesses, and finally, the country. Allowing a system of regional monopolies will exacerbate high healthcare cost, not correct it.

The right policy is to encourage competition with collaboration, not consolidation. We need the dynamic tension of multiple, competing healthcare organizations that also collaborate—coordinating schedules, sharing information and best practices—for the benefit of patients. In this model, care coordination teams compete to be the best in quality outcomes. Whether everyone on the team shares a single employer, or they are independent providers working together under contract, the team with the best quality scores for that patient's condition should win the most business. Everyone competes at the level of the patient experience.

---

35. http://www.aurorahealthcare.org/aboutus/history/default.aspx

Creating and maintaining this balance between collaboration and competition will not be easy. I doubt there are any silver bullets. First, we need to make sure that massive monopolies do not form and blot out regional competition. The Federal Trade Commission has been fairly liberal in granting large mergers, as evidenced by a few of the large corporate health companies out there. On the other hand, the FTC is wary of any agreements between competing organizations on what price to accept for services. Since the 1982 U.S. Supreme Court *Maricopa* decision, this conduct has been considered *per se* unlawful as price fixing. So, how do competing physician groups join together to collaborate on patient care and accept an agreed-upon rate without running afoul of the feds?

A solution may be found in clinical integration. In 1996, the FTC and the Department of Justice issued a Statement of Antitrust Enforcement Policy in Health Care that recognized the public benefit of provider networks created from small practices. These networks collectively negotiate contracts with payers without being accused of price fixing. For instance, the North East Wisconsin Health Value Network (known as NEW HVN) is comprised of independent specialty physicians who work with ThedaCare and Bellin Health Care Systems in Green Bay. Those who belong to NEW HVN work off the same pricing structure and share some resources while being protected from antitrust laws. NEW HVN has an independent administration staff that contracts with insurers and employers, offering a network of physicians that have agreed on a corridor of pricing.[36] Groups operating under the clinical integration ruling—and there are several throughout the country—must show they are engaged in quality tracking and improvement, and that part of physician pay is based on quality scores.

---

36. NEW HVN physicians agree on a corridor of 10–20% discount on fees, for instance, with each small practice controlling the specific discount it offers.

While clinical integration has the right intentions, it does create another layer of bureaucracy. ThedaCare, Bellin, and the physicians who joined all had to spend money to hire a separate NEW HVN administration and pay legal fees to ensure we were operating within FTC rules. This is the kind of waste that adds to healthcare costs. Instead of operating within an exception, like the clinical integration idea, or settling for a simplistic tool like fixed pricing, we need laws that promote collaboration while encouraging competition.

The Smaller Scale

The need for separate and competing organizations does not descend, however, to the level of single practitioners. While most Americans still receive at least part of their healthcare from small or solo practices, medicine is rapidly becoming a team sport. Recent medical school graduates are choosing more often to become employees of existing health systems or join multispecialty practices, just to avoid the tangle of rules and laws that stand between them and their patients. It no longer makes sense that every physician should be his or her own business. It is nothing more than a complicating factor in the care of patients, in most cases.

As for specialists, even those who remain independent will most likely align themselves with one coordinated-care team, which may or may not include a hospital. Maintaining surgical privileges at several hospitals will become harder. This is a trend we have already begun seeing in healthcare, with specialists also making exclusive deals with hospitals to take a share of the savings they help organizations achieve. It just makes sense for physicians to find a big umbrella to shield them from risk.

Smaller or solo practices still exist in many markets, especially in rural areas, and most cannot possibly gather the funding necessary to take on any level of risk. It is unlikely solo practices can continue independent-ly, without being attached somehow to a hospital or multispecialty group, unless special provisions are made within a healthcare redesign. In fact, there should be special incentives for these rural practices to integrate into organizations that can provide the support required to measure and improve quality. Most of these doctors have no clue how their quality and cost measures stack up and they receive little or no feedback to help them stay current or improve performance. Many are happy not to be bothered with measurements and data, but in the new world of better patient value, that is not an option.

Once quality and cost measures are introduced in rural markets, a new issue will arise. Where patient numbers are small, one bad outcome can skew the data and the finances of a practice. These providers will need financial protection, most likely in the form of partnerships with larger organizations that can manage risk and purchase reinsurance. Creative minds will also need to find a way to make sure that a small practice's quality data does not bottom out as the result of one bad outcome.

Urban markets will have their own challenges, especially in the beginning. There is a very good chance that many previously uninsured people—with conditions long untreated—will flood into the system in certain areas. Access will be a critical issue. Even before that happens, however, organizations in larger markets will need to begin preparing for the coming changes.

As pilot programs to test new payment structures begin throughout the country, we need to ensure that enough patients are involved to make significant statements about the effects of the pilot. Healthcare in this country has suffered repeatedly when big decisions are made based on small trials. Fifty knee replacements using bundled payments will not tell us everything we need to know; many hundreds will be required.

Therefore, medical communities in large regional markets will need to step up, organize pilots of bundled payment systems, find ways to entice patients to participate, and publish the results. While we need the cooperation of Medicare and Medicaid in these trials, it is far preferable that the pilots are organized and run by independent health plans, physician groups, and hospitals, simply because the federal government creates programs that are hopelessly rule-bound and take too long to report.

In Wisconsin, where physicians, insurance executives, and state policy makers have already donated thousands of hours to WHIO and the Partnership for Healthcare Payment Reform, we have secured the cooperation of Medicaid—giving us access to thousands of potential patients for early trials. We still have to convince these patients to join, however. Tom Williams of the California-based initiative working on a knee-replacement trial, reports the same concern. His trial includes insurance companies representing 20% of all commercially insured patients in the state, but his group still needs to convince each patient to become part of this experiment.

We also need Medicare patients—and officials—involved in these trials. Medicare patients comprise about 20% of the nation's adult population, and a larger portion of the healthcare dollars spent. To foresee the issues that new payment structures will uncover, we need Medicare data and participation.

Some Immediate Benefits

Here is the good news for healthcare CEOs and patients alike: In this system, health plans and groups will make money by saving money. The money is now in the margins. Add *saving money to transparent quality data* and we should get healthcare leaders with an urgent focus on value. That means healthcare organizations will work harder to remove the waste that gets in the way of good patient care.

Quality care is the most important outcome of healthcare redesign. But I should also point out here that highly coordinated care should result in higher paychecks for good physicians. A single global payment based on fee-for-service components, managed by a coordinated-care team, with less waste and duplication of administrative resources will result in more money for providers. Not only will there be less duplication, a single bundled payment forces providers to come together and look carefully at the resources used by each party in patient treatment. At this point, a knee specialist who bills separately can order the most expensive prosthetic available and a hospital will comply. Working with a team of colleagues, however, who are all personally interested in the bottom line, that same knee specialist will need to justify his choices. Coordinated-care teams accepting bundled payments will need to consider every aspect of the patient experience to reduce waste, such as waiting, duplication of effort, and unnecessarily high costs for supplies.

As teams and hospitals look for saving opportunities, for instance, there will be a big push to lower "bed days." These are expensive days that patients spend in hospital and health plans have been tracking these numbers for years. Organizations will have to reduce upstream waste in the form of errors, poor planning, and the lack of coordination that keeps patients in the hospital longer than necessary, and too often results in return hospital visits due to poorly managed aftercare.

In a definitive study of hospital utilization among health plans, Milliman, Inc. looked at millions of hospital stays and found a wide disparity in these numbers. Loosely managed health plans had 283 bed days per thousand enrollees, according to Milliman's Utilization Model by Degree of Healthcare Management study. A moderately well-managed health plan might pay for just 222 bed days per thousand enrollees. To be a well-managed plan, which Milliman's Jim Schibanoff defines as an aspirational category, bed days per thousand is 162.

"This is a good number to track because the way to achieve a shorter length of stay is not to kick a patient out early—quicker and sicker, as they say. If you do that, a certain number will just come back with complications and more bed days. The point is to improve the process of care so that the quicker discharge is a natural consequence of better care," said Dr. Schibanoff, who is board certified in internal and pulmonary medicine and the editor-in-chief of the widely used *Milliman Care Guidelines*.

Tracking bed days makes sense, but it will not be without controversy. During the HMO backlash, people often complained about "drive-by labor and delivery" and feeling pushed out of care too early.

"Here's a classic example," Dr. Schibanoff said. "In the 1990s, I was working in a hospital that had really refined total hip-replacement procedures. Physicians got the catheter out right after surgery, reducing the risk of infection, and got the patient up and moving the night of surgery to avoid blood clots and deconditioning of the muscles. It was a natural consequence of this care for patients to leave the hospital after three days.

"I gave a talk in New York about this achievement and caused a big uproar. I was nearly accused of elder abuse. The standard hospital stay for hip replacements in New York was a week."

Reducing bed days, done right, will mean better aftercare, not less. In the case of a total hip replacement, for instance, it is less expensive and more effective to send caregivers to the patient's home—such as a nurse to evaluate fall risks, a pharmacist to coordinate medications and answer questions, and a dietician to ensure good nutrition—than it is to keep the patient in hospital, or readmit that patient after a week.

At ThedaCare, a four-year experiment into the effects of coordinated care proved that better patient care and cost savings could happen simultaneously. We will talk more about Collaborative Care in the coming chapters, but let me point out here that the average length of stay in a medical unit at ThedaCare fell from 3.5 days to 2.9 days in a Collaborative Care Unit. Patient satisfaction rose in the new units to 95%, from 68%. And average cost per case dropped by $730 since 2006, while costs on other units rose by nearly $1,200.

There will be new focus on prevention activities for chronic disease patients, as well. This is the biggest opportunity we have to save money while improving patient lives. We—doctors, administrators, the healthcare community—have not been collecting this low-hanging fruit because we did not need to. Everyone was paid by the office visit, by the procedure. Tell physicians their job is to save money by keeping people healthy and by doing that increase their paychecks, and we will see the style of care for chronic patients change dramatically.

 The problem for many organizations is where and how to start these changes. How do we organize care to benefit the patient and save money? That is the subject of the next section, and the true point of this book.

Part III
Patient-Focused Healthcare

Chapter 10

Patient-Centered Care

I t was mid-summer 2010 when the full scope of everything that Nancy D'Agostino did not know hit home. Still raw from surgery and missing parts of her body, she thought that all the hard choices were behind her. Then here was a new face, a radiation oncologist, outlining side effects of treatment and asking her to choose. And then a medical oncologist was offering chemotherapy and everyone was saying treatment was her choice.

"I have a BA in sociology, for heaven's sake," D'Agostino said. "I'm a smart person, but I was having a hard time absorbing what they were saying."

There had not been a lot of time to study up on the subject, either. In mid-June, she went in for her annual mammogram and told the nurse about a small lump on top of her left breast that she discovered in the shower a few days earlier. D'Agostino's mammogram was read immediately and a doctor suggested she get an ultrasound next. They could do it right away. Impressed with the office efficiency and with one eye on the clock because she had a carpool of girls to collect from the ice rink, D'Agostino agreed. There was definitely a shadow in her breast; a solid form that nobody liked.

D'Agostino's family doctor was part of a multispecialty clinic that did a lot of testing on site, so they could also offer D'Agostino an ultrasound-guided needle biopsy of the tumor immediately. Across town, skating practice was winding down so D'Agostino consented to this next step so long as they promised to make it quick.

"I literally went from exam to biopsy in an hour," D'Agostino recalled. "Then I was back in the car with six girls and their skating bags, holding an ice bag to my chest and it hit me: I just had a bad mammogram. I'm 43, I've got two kids and a husband and a carpool and I really don't have time for this. I cried a little."

Two days later, while packing for a family Father's Day trip, she got the news that it was cancer. Monday morning, accompanied by her husband, D'Agostino met her surgeon and connected with her immediately. Dr. Honnie Bermas answered her questions, scheduled more tests, and outlined D'Agostino's choices. Lumpectomy or mastectomy? One breast or both? D'Agostino needed to choose a plastic surgeon and a hospital.

Over the next week, overwhelmed and feeling like she had been hit by a truck, D'Agostino felt alone. Just before the July 4 holiday, she met a girlfriend for lunch at an Olive Garden restaurant who looked at D'Agostino aghast and said, "Why haven't you ripped that thing out by now?"

"She was right," D'Agostino said. "I wanted no part of that tumor. I wanted nothing to come back that would hurt me. I wanted nothing left behind."

Having decided on a bilateral mastectomy with immediate reconstruction work, D'Agostino felt relieved. A month after her diagnosis, she was in Appleton Medical Center for dual surgeries and out again 24 hours later. She was prepared to focus on her recovery.

She was not prepared for the medical oncologist or the radiation oncologist and a completely new set of life-and-death decisions. "They started talking about percentages and life expectancy and they wanted a decision from me, but I was lost," D'Agostino said. "I was two weeks post surgery. Parts of my body were missing. The easiest thing was to do nothing. That's what I wanted."

Nothing was what she almost got—not because it was the best thing for D'Agostino, but because of the way systems of care at Appleton Medical Center was arranged.

More than 200,000 women are diagnosed with breast cancer every year. According to the National Cancer Institute, one in every eight women born today will be diagnosed with breast cancer in her lifetime. For those of us working in healthcare, this is familiar territory and a patient should benefit from our prior experience. We know, for instance, that questions about chemotherapy will most likely follow a mastectomy, but we did not prepare Nancy for what we knew was coming. If a medical team lacks coordination, the patient lacks the benefit of all preceding cases.

Without coordination, a patient can languish for weeks from one step to the next while her tumor grows and the illness progresses. Without integrated care, critical information is easily lost and treatment delayed or misdirected. Or, as happened to D'Agostino, specialists offer complex and sometimes contradictory information to the patient who sorts it out alone.

Lack of coordination exists, as I have said earlier, because systems have been set up to benefit physicians. Doctors are busy people. They tell themselves that they must organize their patients for maximum efficiency in order to get everything done. If that means visiting a hospitalized patient before dawn, when the patient is too groggy to communicate effectively, so be it. If an important surgery needs to wait a week until the doctor is doing three other similar surgeries —that is business as usual.

In the world of lean thinking, this is called batch processing. The operator (doctor) lines up the work in progress (patients) that require similar activities and then performs that task on each in succession. Manufacturing and service companies that convert to lean thinking have realized that batch processing creates a focus too narrow. Waste and inventory accumulate between discrete operations; communication failures become endemic. When an operator's job is one small piece, he or she easily loses sight of the complete product and hence, the customer's needs. The customer, after all, is paying for a whole product, not the individual pieces.

Here is a classic example of batch processing in medicine: At ThedaCare, it used to be the practice in Labor & Delivery for nurses to line up all the newborns that needed a first check-up, allowing the doctor is simply move down the line, performing examinations. It makes sense, right? But not for the patient or the newborn's parents. When a multidisciplinary improvement team gathered to consider the value stream of a family's progress through Labor & Delivery, the team realized that performing that newborn examination in seclusion meant new parents were missing a valuable opportunity to discuss any lingering concerns or findings with the doctor. In at least one incident, there were tragic consequences.

As ThedaCare began a transformation to lean thinking in 2002, one of the most important breakthroughs came as leaders realized that the core product was not surgical procedures or physician consultations or IV bags and bandages. That is what most healthcare providers thought they were selling. What people wanted to buy, however, was healthcare—babies safely delivered, mended bones, tumors removed, better heart function.

Improving the Patient's Journey

Like St. Boniface in Winnipeg, Canada, Seattle Children's Hospital, and Group Health of Puget Sound in Washington, and other organizations, ThedaCare has been using lean thinking to redesign the way everyone in the system looks at healthcare. This work has helped hospitals and caregivers remove waste from the system, cut costs, and improve quality. The revolutionary facet of lean, however, has been the way it taught people to organize work to the patient's needs, to see from the patient's point of view.

Using lean methods, ThedaCare and others created teams to investigate the way a patient moves through the journey of care and then improve it. Lean improvement teams usually include a dozen or so members—physicians, nurses, pharmacists, patients, administrators, and complete outsiders—that have a week to investigate a situation, decide on and make improvements. The work begins with mapping everything that happens to a patient in order to see the value stream. Every contact a patient has with a staff member, every motion the staff member makes to provide care, every aspirin offered—or not—is noted.

Value-stream mapping is often a humbling experience for healthcare providers. In general, patients move from one silo to the next: imaging, labs, specialists, nursing, pharmacy, and rehabilitation. Most healthcare improvement focuses on optimizing the performance of each silo, independent of the others. Waste and error mostly occur between the silos, however, as the patient is passed from one unit to the next. In engineering, they refer to the practice of processing one element at a time and then moving it to the next silo as "throwing it over the wall." A design engineer might make a drawing, for instance, and then throw it over the wall to manufacturing engineers, without consultation or feedback. It is a terrible image, but that is what we were doing: throwing patients over the wall.

Nancy D'Agostino hit the gap in ThedaCare's system after her surgery. While she trusted Dr. Bermas, she only met with the surgeon once after her operation. Next, according to her treatment plan, D'Agostino needed to meet with oncologists and make some critical decisions, but nobody prepared her for that. She was simply thrown over the wall.

With encouragement from her family and friends, D'Agostino sought another opinion from a treatment group in Milwaukee. There, she met with radiation and medical oncologists again and heard some new numbers. If she had chemotherapy as opposed to nothing, she learned, the chance that her muscinous carcinoma would return dropped from 20% to 10%. Being relatively young, she was assured she could get through chemotherapy without too much trouble. The medical oncologist in Milwaukee was so convinced that D'Agostino would benefit, he called D'Agostino's husband while she was driving home and outlined, again, the benefits. D'Agostino returned to Appleton Medical Center for treatment in the Cancer Center.

Fortunately, improvement teams had begun value-stream mapping the flow of breast cancer patients through the system and preparing to remake the system. So, when D'Agostino told a nurse one day that their signage was terrible and left patients confused about where to go, the nurse thanked her profusely and invited her to join a Rapid Improvement Event as the most important voice on the team: the patient.

Following the Map

Let's leave the nascent improvement work in the Cancer Center for a moment in order to see the full scope of value-stream mapping and continuous improvement in a healthcare setting. Beginning in 2006, ThedaCare teams documented everything that happened to a patient who arrived at an Emergency Room with chest pains. Value-stream maps showed a confusion of duplicated efforts, wasted time, and potential for error.

If a patient with chest pains was having a rather common ST segment elevated myocardial infarction (STEMI), doctors and nurses had about 90 minutes to get her diagnosed and prepared, get a team in place, and snake a catheter into her femoral artery and inflate a balloon to clear the blockage and return blood flow to her heart. When the process takes more than 90 minutes, the chances of irreversible damage to the heart muscle skyrocketed. While ThedaCare had been repeatedly named the best organization in Wisconsin and one of the best in the country for treating heart attacks, the truth was that patients were getting angioplasty within 90 minutes just 65% of the time.

By mapping everything that happened to a STEMI patient and then removing the now-obvious waste—such as a duplicative diagnosis between emergency physicians and cardiologists—the improvement team could attack one issue at a time. Over the course of a year, teams removed waste, implemented new standard procedures, and trained ER personnel in new methods until it took an average of just 37 minutes to get a STEMI patient from the hospital doors to a life-saving balloon angioplasty.

Using the lean discipline of continuous improvement, new teams took that STEMI work and duplicated it throughout the system and into the far reaches of ThedaCare's treatment areas. When a patient develops a clutching chest pain anywhere in northeast Wisconsin now, ThedaCare teams can reliably deliver that patient for angioplasty—including helicopter or ambulance travel—to surgery within 90 minutes.

Using value-stream mapping in the Cancer Center, teams also discovered that patients like D'Agostino were alone and unprepared for the big questions and new decisions that had to be made. Specialists were not aligned. Because of Rapid Improvement Events, surgeons, oncologists, general practitioners, plastic surgeons, behavioral health counselors, and others began meeting in weekly conferences—some of them joining by video link—to discuss current cases. With counselors in the room, the team is encouraged to discuss all aspects of the patient, her situation, and her needs. In addition, two new care coordinators were added to the Cancer Center to guide women through the process from surgery to recovery, making sure every patient is fully informed and prepared for the next step.

The New Delivery Model

As Nancy D'Agostino's story illustrates, healthcare providers universally do some things right and some things wrong. It is natural for people and organizations to focus on the "right things," but that will not get us anywhere. In a medical situation, things done wrong can lead to injury and death. As painful as it can be, providers absolutely need to focus on organizational errors. We need to see the process from the patient's point of view, recognize defects, create avenues to fix those defects, and train our people to do it every single day. The goal, no matter how lofty it may seem, is always zero errors. It requires constant perseverance and a robust method of problem-solving that everyone can use.

Lean healthcare organizations have found the method, and the perseverance, through a culture of continuous improvement. It requires a commitment of time and resources and at it is not cheap. At ThedaCare, at least a half-dozen improvement teams have been at work every single week in areas throughout the organization since 2002. Every team is fully empowered—and expected—to make changes for the benefit of patients. Teams report every Friday on what they accomplished during the week, not what they recommend.

Meanwhile, four letters dominate staff meetings in every unit of ThedaCare hospitals: PDSA. Plan, Do, Study, Act is the application of the scientific method to all problems. If errors occur in patient care, staff members do not seek out a guilty person and cast blame. Ninety-nine percent of the time, the process, not people, causes error. So, staff members create a plan to study the problem, decide on a course of action, and implement the solution. This cycle can last 10 minutes, two weeks, or two years. The point is to find and correct the systemic error, and to keep people focused on finding and fixing problems.

Lean work has required changes in the way healthcare professionals think—to embrace the fact that change is constant and improvement should be, and to adopt a more egalitarian working style. At ThedaCare, physicians are no longer the center of gravity or the final authority.

Beginning in 2007, with a grant from the Robert Wood Johnson Foundation administered by the Institute for Healthcare Improvement, a core team of nurses, physicians, pharmacists, social workers, and administrators began a six-month investigation into what a truly patient-focused hospital unit would be. The team considered the current model, in which physicians control patient care and leave barely legible orders without consulting colleagues, and decided it was not working. Too many people were out of the loop and doctors were running from one quick consultation to another with barely enough time to answer questions.

The team used cardboard and spare parts to redesign patient rooms, nursing stations, and hospital units. Team members wanted nurses to spend less time waiting for instructions or running around looking for supplies. Doctors should lead care teams, they said, not operate solo. They wanted to include pharmacists at the point-of-care in order to reduce medication reconciliation errors, which are the root of most patient harm. In short, they wanted to break up the system of silos and, in that spirit, named the unit Collaborative Care.

In late 2007, the Collaborative Care pilot site in Appleton Medical Center opened for business. The redesigned unit was a large square with every patient room visible from a central cluster of meeting areas where teams of doctors, nurses, and pharmacists gathered daily to update every patient's progress and current needs. Patient rooms were equipped with a closet that included all supplies, both general and specific to the patient needs. The closets were designed with rollout shelves accessible from outside the room, so patients were not disturbed by housekeeping and restocking.

In this unit, the full care team—physician, nurse, pharmacist, and social workers, if needed—met with a patient and family within 90 minutes of admittance to create a plan of care. The nurse then took over as case manager, responsible for administering the plan and preparing the patient for each new step. The patient's expected release date was written on a large board in the room, encouraging all caregivers to think ahead and eliminate the hectic final tests and quick consultations that often occur before a patient is sent home.

Morning rounds take more time in Collaborative Care and some physicians had a hard time accepting that. Those who stuck with it, however, said that the new model might mean a few more minutes spent with care teams each morning, but they enjoyed a significant decrease in follow-up telephone calls. Questions and concerns were answered on the spot, which meant patients were getting the right care more quickly and doctors were spending less time answering calls later in the day.

The results of the Collaborative Care experiment have been astounding. Medication reconciliation errors—which result in under- and overdosing due to miscommunication about what drugs the patient is actually taking—used to average more than one for every patient chart. In Collaborative Care units, medication reconciliation errors were eliminated by the end of 2008 and remain at zero. Quality of pneumonia care went from hitting 38% of quality markers to 100% consistently. Patient satisfaction was 95% in 2010.[37] When ThedaCare board members saw the results, including the fact that cost of care was 30% less than in traditional units, they decided to convert all hospital beds to Collaborative Care.

ThedaCare's primary care clinics have been going through similar conversions. Using value-stream maps, continuous improvement teams, and a new focus on patient experience, ThedaCare has reduced wait times and waiting rooms, added on-site laboratories for test results in 15 minutes and empowered physician assistants to take more responsibility in coordinating care.

The results of this work are well illustrated at the Kimberly Clinic, where four general-practice physicians embraced continuous improvement teams beginning in 2006. At Kimberly, patients can get same-day appointments when needed. They spend an average five minutes in the waiting room and 75–80% of the time, the doctor arrives in the exam room within five minutes of the patient. Laboratory results are slipped under the door within 15 minutes of testing. Every patient leaves with a plan of care, explaining what medications changed or stopped, time of next appointment, if necessary, and any follow-up actions required. Change has also been good for the bottom line. In 2006, the Kimberly Clinic lost a typical $400,000. In 2009, for the first time, the clinic turned a profit.

The new delivery model has refocused the attention of providers, dramatically cut costs, and improved quality outcomes rapidly. These results are great, but I have begun to envision loftier goals. I want to change what patients demand of their providers, to create a completely new set of expectations. In the next chapter, we will look at the path to more universal improvements.

---

37. Meaning that 95% of responding patients gave the experience at ThedaCare a perfect score of 5 out of 5.

Chapter 11

Changing
Expectations

Better healthcare will change us. As patients, as family of patients, our expectations will rise along with the quality ratings of our hospitals and physicians. Once patients have seen processes with zero defects, that will be the standard demanded. Patients will have sharp questions for anything less than perfect care. Does this sound frightening?

For a market-based, quality-driven healthcare system to work, sharp questions are necessary. In the same way that patients and their needs *should be* at the center of all healthcare processes, patient demands must be the engine and focus of healthcare's direction. This will inevitably alter the doctor-patient relationship. The old *Marcus Welby* doctor-knows-best paradigm will someday look just as absurd as television news anchors smoking cigarettes during a broadcast.

Most doctors already report seeing a change in behavior. A certain percentage of patients arrive for consultations now with treatment studies or new research gleaned from the Internet. This is a good first step toward an equal relationship, but none of us yet has enough clear, actionable data to enable a truly level playing field.

Most physicians have mixed feelings about this change in relationship, I know. Many doctors look forward to the day that informed patients come to them as partners, seeking advice while bringing their own information and ideas to the consultation. But even these progressive doctors acknowledge that absolute trust—even a little hero worship—from their patients will be hard to give up. The change will be more difficult for physicians who enjoy a sense of control, who only ask that patients show up for their scheduled surgery on time.

Change will be difficult for patients, too, said Dr. Michael Ray, a radiation oncologist who left his teaching post and practice at the University of Michigan for a practice in Appleton. "Coming from Ann Arbor to Appleton, I was struck by the number of patients who are dependent on doctor opinions here," Dr. Ray said. "Sometimes, you can offend or shock patients if you try to engage them on the level of choice. I've had patients tell me, 'You're the expert, you make the decision.'"

Changing the doctor-patient relationship in order to engage critical thinking and consumerism in patients will probably take a generation or more, and we should be prepared for that. Just think about how long it took to affect smoking as a cultural norm. In 1965, when research had already established a firm link between smoking and lung cancer, 42% of U.S. adults smoked. Tobacco was heavily entrenched in the public's imagination of what it meant to be a sophisticated adult or a rebellious teenager. Decades of health warnings and public education ensued. Cigarettes were heavily taxed and, state by state, banned from public areas—each new restriction causing a fresh uproar. New campaigns are still launched every year to pressure moviemakers to eliminate smoking from films, or to inform smoking parents of the dangers of second-hand smoke. Still, more than 20% of people smoke.

A blind-trust relationship between doctors and patients does not have the carcinogenic bite of cigarettes, but it is dangerous to the system because we need patients asking questions, making judgments, and forcing us through competition to be better providers. In effect, we need a nation of scientists and it is up to us to help everyone rise to that level.

In a nation with high school graduation rates at 70% and college degrees held by 56% of the population, creating a nation of scientists may sound daunting. It underscores, however, the critical need for item one on a healthcare redesign agenda: transparency of quality and cost measures, published in a clear, concise, and easily accessible manner. We will need public education campaigns to help people understand the importance of this data and learn to read it, just as we informed people of the dangers of smoking.

Once people have full access to data—and understand it—they will become better partners in their own healthcare. Equally critical, informed patients will also keep the healthcare system pushing toward better quality outcomes through competition.

We should not, however, expect perfect patients. There will always be some percentage of people who make their own decisions, independent of doctor's advice or medical research. Another percentage of the patient population will always lean too heavily on his or her physician, abdicating all personal decision-making responsibility. But most patients belong to a majority middle group: those who engage in independent research and mix it with a physician's advice. These patients need encouragement, and must be supported with information that is useful, timely, and digestible by anyone with a high school education.

Beyond quality and cost data on clinics and individual providers, the majority of patients also need access to the best evidence-based research on conditions and treatments. We need to do a better job of publishing medical research in language accessible to the general population. This means potential patients will need to learn—probably in high school—how to weigh different studies and ask critical questions that need to be applied to any new research.

Why We Need to Know

Consider, for instance, prostate cancer. One man in every six will be diagnosed with prostate cancer in his lifetime, according to the American Cancer Society. More than two million men in the United States are living with this diagnosis and recent studies have indicated that nearly every man who lives long enough will eventually develop the disease. Prostate cancer is ubiquitous, and yet men receive wildly different information and advice, depending on where they receive treatment.

Many health organizations strongly recommend that all men 50 and older receive annual prostate cancer screenings. Early detection can lead to simpler, more effective treatment. Or, regular screening can lead to false positives and unnecessary treatment. Some prostate cancer will never seriously affect a man's health, whereas treatment can have side effects such as incontinence and impotence. The Centers for Disease Control reports that there is insufficient evidence to recommend for or against regular screening.[38] Every man needs to make his own informed decision about screening, which means that every man must understand his options and make critical choices long before a diagnosis.

---

38. In late 2011, the U.S. Preventive Services Task Force recommended against all PSA screening, stating that general screening led to more needless tests and treatments than lives saved.

A man who opts for regular screening—usually through a prostate-specific antigen (PSA) test—and has a suddenly elevated PSA reading can face a confusing array of choices for treatment after a biopsy confirms cancer: surgery, radiation seed therapy, freezing, hormone therapy, external radiation, or watchful waiting.

A study of nearly 12,000 men published in the *Journal of Clinical Oncology*[39] confirmed what many physicians long suspected. Collecting data from 36 clinical sites, the study asked what type of treatment men were choosing. About 50% chose surgery to remove the prostate; 14% chose androgen deprivation monotherapy, commonly known as hormone therapy; 13% opted for radiation seed therapy; nearly 12% had external beam radiation; 7% chose watchful waiting; 4% chose cryoablation.[40] If disease truly drove treatment as it should, and these treatments reflected the best options for various levels of disease, we would expect to see these percentages reflected steadily across the clinical sites with only minor variations. Instead, treatment patterns varied markedly across the clinical sites in a way that could not be explained by case-mix variability. One site, for instance, showed a surprising 74% of patients chose cryoablation.

"We know that the treatment you get mostly depends on who you see," said Jack Swanson, MD, a medical oncologist for 15 years before taking over the palliative care program at ThedaCare. "Surgeons are mostly interested in surgery. And I'm sure that, deep down, surgeons really believe that surgery is the way to go. But if the surgeon sees that, due to circumstances like age and health, radiation is the way to go, that patient should be referred to a radiation oncologist. That rarely happens, though."

---

39. "Time Trends and Local Variation in Primary Treatment of Localized Prostate Cancer," by Matthew R. Cooperberg, Jeanette M. Broering, and Peter Carroll, *Journal of Clinical Oncology*, Vol. 28, March 2010.
40. The use of extreme cold to kill and remove tissue, such as the prostate.

Dr. Ray, the radiation oncologist, admits that his bias would be toward radiation therapy. To be fair, he said, the best option would be to offer patients a multispecialty conference consultation.

"Patients need help sorting it through and that's the most valuable thing we do—putting complicated medical issues into plain English," Dr. Ray said. "A lot of physicians don't have the time or motivation to do that, however. They're only rewarded for procedures."

Patients who know they have a choice, and are aware of the financial ramifications of the decisions they make, will likely demand more information. And the healthcare centers that offer services like a multi-specialty consultation for prostate cancer patients, will be judged as having better quality.

The question is, do we really trust patients to make their own decisions?

Giving Patients Choice

Every doctor has stories about patients who demand expensive treatments well past the time it makes sense. There will always be men battling late-stage incurable cancer who want more chemotherapy, just to feel like they are still in the fight. As there will be women with chronic disease—blind and without legs, due to years of diabetes—who still opt for dialysis three times a week.

Other people will look at the research studies showing that people who receive palliative care instead of aggressive treatments live months longer,[41] and that patients who choose hospice care live about a month

---

41. In a study published in the *New England Journal of Medicine*, August 2010, researchers at Massachusetts General Hospital found that lung cancer patients receiving early palliative care experienced less depression, better quality of life, and lived 2.7 months longer than those receiving cancer treatment alone.

longer than those who do not,[42] and select this less expensive route of comfort care.

Choice of treatment, I believe, belongs to the fully informed patient. By "fully informed," I mean patients who understand the risks and consequences, and who know the costs. Like many medical professionals, I believe that patients need to pay a share of the cost of healthcare and know the cost of every procedure, in order to be truly informed.

Even patients without skin in the game, however, make better decisions for their lives when given information and options. Informed patients who understand the ramifications of aggressive treatment versus conservative approaches mostly choose the most noninvasive options.

The most comprehensive studies regarding patient choice and aggressive treatment have been related to end-of-life directives. In few other areas of medicine do physicians have such open-ended discussions with patients about options, without the intent to direct patients on a particular course of treatment. In a 2008 study published in the *Journal of the American Medical Association*, researchers reported that terminally ill cancer patients who had end-of-life discussions with their doctors experienced fewer hospitalizations, less time in an ICU, and had better quality-of-life scores on a standardized survey. Additionally, the patients' main caregivers—usually a family member— reported fewer major depressive disorders and better adjustment to bereavement when end-of-life discussions took place. An adjusted analysis showed more aggressive treatment was associated with worse quality of life for the patient (6.4 versus 4.6).[43]

---

42. A study of 4,493 Medicare patients, published in the *Journal of Pain and Symptom Management*, March 2007, showed that terminally ill patients who received hospice services lived, on average, 29 days longer than those who did not.
43. Alexi A. Wright, MD, Baohui Zhang, MD, Alaka Ray, MD, et al, "Associations Between End of Life Discussions, Patient Mental Health, Medical Care Near Death, and Caregiver Bereavement Adjustment," JAMA, October 2008, Vol. 300, No. 14

Another study of 3,321 veterans hospitalized with advanced disease in 2004–2006 showed that total hospital costs were $464 a day lower for the 18% of patients who chose palliative care, which includes those big discussions.[44] The group that received palliative care was 43.7% less likely to be admitted to an ICU during hospitalization than patients receiving the usual care.[45]

We cannot expect physicians to change overnight, however. Physicians will always have a bias to treat symptoms and diseases, even if that can cause a diminished quality of life. We have a deep-seated need to tell patients that we can fix their problems. For many doctors, conversations that involve acceptance of mortality feel like failure. So, we send patients out for another MRI or CT scan even if it is unnecessary,[46] another round of testing, and hope that a new treatment will become available instead of simply talking to our patients about what lies ahead.

"I think doctors are getting a little better about not saying we can keep you going forever and ever," said Dr. Swanson. "A little better. But if we start to pay doctors and hospitals the right way—not to do things, but to manage diseases—then the discussions would be a lot different. We don't want to go back to the HMO way, which was to pay doctors for *not* doing things. We need financial incentives lined up with helping people have quality lives and good end-of-life experiences. If we were paid right, these would be very different consultations."

---

44. Palliative care focuses on lessening the severity of disease symptoms and providing comfort to the patient, instead of halting the course of disease.

45. Joan D. Penron, Ph.D., Partha Deb, Ph.D., Cornelia Dellenbaugh, et al., "Hospital-Based Palliative Care Consultation: Effects on Hospital Costs," *Journal of Palliative Medicine*, November 2010, Vol. 13

46. The most common estimate is that 35–40% of MRIs and CT scans are unnecessary, as well as costly. In a 2009 special report, CBS Evening News reported that unnecessary scans add about $35 billion to the nation's annual healthcare costs.

    At Virginia Mason Hospital and Medical Center in Seattle, a collaborative team that redesigned the care delivery process for uncomplicated back pain found that a simple mistake-proofing process for ordering MRIs dramatically lowered the incidence of unnecessary tests. After creating the Virginia Mason Spine Clinic to focus on treatment of common back pain, team members reported that between 2004 and 2007, MRIs at the clinic decreased by 31% even while patient satisfaction shot up to about 98%.

In my own practice as an internist, I would diagnose diseases and send patients to treatment experts. My patients often came back to me, confused at their choices, full of questions and without really understanding how treatment would affect their lives and well-being. All these patients knew was that one expert had prescribed X procedure and maybe another doctor prescribed Y. My patients did not really have a voice or a choice in their treatment, I saw, because they were not fully informed.

Patients need us to fully disclose quality and cost information. They need our unbiased opinions. They need a system that supports and guides them through treatment. And then, patients need to make choices and take responsibility.

This healthcare system will demand that patients and physicians assume new roles, with more responsibility and a greater sense of collaboration. This reality begs a question. Physicians have long enjoyed economic and cultural status in this country. Why would they want a new role? Let's look at how providers can benefit from a new healthcare system.

Chapter 12

What's in it
for Providers?

A t healthcare conferences and site visits around the country where I talk about improving quality and lowering costs with lean thinking, I see worried faces. In every crowd, there are skeptics and enthusiasts, but one burning question unites physicians: What kind of future do we have, post redesign?

Physicians worry that huge medical bills will be settled on their backs. They worry about losing professional freedom and economic status if the government runs healthcare. They worry that skimpy public funding will leave them unable to care properly for patients.

This is why I advocate for a competition-based, free-market healthcare system. The future that I see for lean healthcare providers is one of financial health and stability, with happier patients and more engaged staff members. We have already seen this happening at ThedaCare and other lean healthcare systems. It is not the easiest path, but lean thinking offers the only intelligent answer to our goal: better healthcare at a price we can afford.

Show Me the Money

The time of endlessly increasing revenue is over. Physicians and healthcare leaders have relied too much on a strategy of revenue growth in recent years. We would buy a new gizmo or gadget—more advanced MRI machines or the latest in robotic surgery equipment—enabling us to charge more and, hopefully, grow market share by advertising new capabilities. With healthcare fast approaching 20% of the nation's gross domestic product, however, this strategy is unsustainable. The nation cannot afford us.

Actual revenue for the healthcare system will decrease. We all see this coming. The questions are how we will live in the new reality and who will take the hit.

The answer is in the value stream. Organizations that see the value streams by which we deliver healthcare to patients, end to end, and learn to identify and remove waste will survive. Those that understand we are paid to maximize the health of patients will thrive.

Achieving financial stability in the new reality will mean removing waste from the system faster than revenue drops. When organizations reduce the cost of care, there will be money left over. When quality improves, there are fewer complications, infections, and readmissions due to error. When we perform fewer unnecessary procedures, less duplicative tests and consultations, wasted time and money is returned to the bottom line. The money, again, is in the margins.

ThedaCare's decade of experiments with continuous improvement proved there was a minimum 30% waste in our healthcare processes. Often, the wasted time, energy, and materials in a process was closer to 50%. These experiments have been repeated in dozens of healthcare organizations in the United States, Canada, and elsewhere with the same results.

The United States spends $2.5 trillion in healthcare every year. The 30-percent-waste in healthcare estimate is widely accepted. That means healthcare waste equals $750 billion every year. So, there is *a lot* of money in the margin.

Organizations that aggressively remove waste and redesign care-delivery systems will be the ones able to pay physicians, nurses, and therapists better wages. (Likewise, healthcare professionals who take the most waste out of care processes will be highly prized.) In the end, the improvement-focused systems will be able to attract the brightest talent.

Existing finance mechanisms and vertical silos, however, are deeply entrenched in our healthcare systems. Moving to new compensation techniques that support healthcare value will require some trial and error.

In the 1980s, for instance, large health systems experimented with capitation in HMOs. It was soon clear that risk was not well apportioned. Family practitioners—also known as the gatekeepers—were paid to keep patients well and they assumed the risk for case management. Specialists, however, were still charging fees for service. Family practitioners who needed to refer patients to a specialist took the brunt of the risk, but were unable to manage system costs. From this, we learned that capitation needed to be system-wide instead of isolated to gatekeepers.

As complicated as healthcare compensation can seem, there are a limited number of workable models that need testing. At an Institute of Medicine Roundtable on Value and Science-Driven Healthcare presented at the Pew Charitable Trusts in June 2011, leaders identified 11 payment reform models. Some of those models, such as payment for performance and payment for shared decision-making, were steps too small. Two of the models focused on "payment adjustments" to limit paying doctors and hospitals for fixing medical errors. But Medicare has already established new rules in which hospitals will not be paid to do rework. If a patient is readmitted within 30 days of discharge with a recurrence of a condition deemed preventable, the hospital is not paid. Medicare is also instituting a few payment "carrots" such as extra pay for doctors completing orders using a computer. These adjustments to the payment system may act as temporary bridges to prepare providers for larger change, but I do not believe they are particularly meaningful in the larger scheme of things.

Meaningful change will come as we study shared savings, bundled payment, and global payment systems. These redesigns will change a doctor's life and practice. I believe we need to focus testing on global and bundled payments, shared savings, care coordination with primary physicians and outcomes-based payment.

Ultimately, I believe that global payments should be the goal. There are still issues to work out, however. When a single, up-front fee is paid to cover the cost of treatment, providers are vulnerable to surprise. Many practices could not handle being hit with two cancers and a heart attack in a short time among a patient population. Testing of a global payment system, therefore, should include experiments with reinsurance agreements and other cost mitigators currently used in the insurance industry.

To find the most workable model, we need to return to the scientific method—observation, hypothesis, testing, and modification of hypothesis or action. Before one payment type will emerge as the clear winner, we need regional health systems to conduct experiments with global and bundled payment for health episodes, and shared savings models. Experiments need to begin now, with reports published in peer-reviewed journals, giving everyone in the medical community an opportunity to see the evidence and join the debate.

Patients and Staff

The scientific method is a comfort zone for most physicians. We like demonstrable facts. This is one reason lean thinking has worked so well in healthcare: We use the scientific method to improve processes. And as a result, we improve working conditions for staff and medical outcomes for patients.

Consider for a moment the unimproved work situation for most nurses and assistants. Already second-tier in status to doctors, most nurses and assistants spend their days running around looking for supplies, charts, and answers to questions. They deliver errors through lack of information or misinformation and take it personally. They are too often shamed and blamed for errors that occur in the process and they lack the authority to fix problems. It is a job that burns people out.

Patients, meanwhile, are the recipients of those errors. Patients are asked the same question multiple times; they get the wrong medications or the wrong doses; they are forgotten, waiting in rooms or on gurneys in the hallway.

In a lean environment, physicians and staff use the scientific method to guide their work in the form of PDSA—plan, do, study, act. Instead of searching for a person to blame, they use PDSA to study the cause of error, devise a plan to correct the system—which is usually at the root of error—and then fix the process. This means that errors must be laid bare for everyone to see, as opposed to hidden. This is another type of transparency demanded in a lean environment. When everyone knows that errors exposed are actually opportunities to improve the system through PDSA instead of avenues to shame, people are less likely to hide their errors and compound problems.

When physicians and staff work PDSA together to find and fix problems, there has been a positive effect on job satisfaction scores at ThedaCare. We found a significant increase in job satisfaction scores after employees participated in three Rapid Improvement Events. Measured from 2005, when ThedaCare made a significant push to incorporate lean thinking and PDSA work throughout the organization, to 2008, overall job satisfaction scores rose from 4.5 to 5.03 on a 6-point scale.

Going beyond simple satisfaction, ThedaCare started focusing deeper, asking five questions on each survey that tried to address how engaged employees were with their jobs and with ThedaCare. We know that "happy" or "satisfied" are not always the defining characteristics of people who are truly engaged in improving their environment. And these are the people we most want to encourage—the game-changers and critical thinkers.

ThedaCare has not been as diligent in conducting physician surveys, but I can report that over a time that included a lot of disruption due to new care-delivery processes and a national economic meltdown, physician job satisfaction scores did not significantly change. Between 2007 and 2010, the overall average bounced around between 3.11 and 3.17 on a 4-point scale.

Anecdotally, I know that most physicians approve of the fact that ThedaCare has been working hard to improve patient care. Those physicians who have been affected most—who have had teams investigate their practices, remove waste, and improve responsiveness—love the new way or, in the case of a very small percentage, they left the organization.

The physicians who stayed reported that they have been able to significantly reduce or eliminate take-home work, they have better support from nurses and assistants, and patients are happier with service.

The Bottom Line

Physicians who embrace lean thinking, who become adept at spotting waste, removing it, and improving patient experiences will be the real winners in the rapidly shifting healthcare economy. These will be the sought-after doctors, whether the payment system model is shared savings, global, or episode group payment.

Even the doctors who simply learn the concepts and become team players instead of autocratic leaders will benefit from stable incomes, more engaged staff, and happier patients. Physicians in a lean environment find that work is more streamlined and there is a much better chance of being home on time.

To achieve this, leading-edge physicians need to join with patients, payers, and policy-makers to change the system. In the next chapter, I will describe the roles that every party needs to play.

Chapter 13

Prescriptions

There is no single or simple answer to achieving a sustainable, quality healthcare system in this country. There is, however, a path on which to begin. I believe that every organization seeking to provide healthcare that is future-relevant must work toward transparency, linking payment to better health outcomes, and focusing all care-delivery systems on the patients' needs. Patients must be able to make rational choices based on accurate information. Payers must support the system by directing their dollars toward the organizations that are transparent, show quality outcomes, and cost-effectiveness.

Everyone has a role to play in making these changes. In this chapter, I will outline crucial moves for each group in the healthcare system: physicians, patients, payers, and policy-makers. Like most prescriptions, this one is given with the full knowledge that there are other choices, other treatment plans out there. Based on my experience—on the experiments I have carried out and observed, and on more than two decades working in and leading healthcare organizations—I believe that this is right path and we must move forward together.

Physicians

Physicians face the most disruptive changes. For 5,000 years—since the Egyptians began attempting disease intervention rather than making sacrifices to shrines—doctors have been paid for doing procedures. Even barbers in the Middle Ages were paid by how many leeches they applied, no matter the outcome. Doctors have enjoyed a high and often mystical status in society throughout history. Many resist changes to healthcare out of fear of losing that status.

To maintain their position as trusted leaders, however, physicians now need to get out in front on healthcare redesign. Beginning in their own practices, physicians need to organize care around the needs of their patients, learn to recognize waste—what the patient *does not* need—and eliminate it. Surgeons, internists, and other specialists working in hospitals need to work with administrators and staff to map and understand the entire value stream of the patient experience. Considering the way in which medicine has fragmented into so many specialties, doctors can no longer imagine that they are the sum total of the patient experience.

While working with others to improve the patient experience, physicians will need to become team members instead of independent autocrats. Good doctors will still maintain a special position on health-care teams in light of their advanced knowledge and ability to share that with others. But the day of the cowboy doctor who rides in on a white horse, scribbles down some instructions, and rides off into the landscape are numbered. In an environment where professionals work the scientific method—PDSA—together to improve care, that cowboy doctor is an anachronism.

Standardizing care and emphasizing evidence-based care guidelines will help these team efforts. When nurses and assistants are trained to use care guidelines, they become more adept at seeing issues before they arise and planning better care for patients. Support staff becomes more valuable to physicians when equipped with these tools.

Some doctors still deride evidence-based care as "cookie-cutter medicine" and fear that care guidelines and standardized processes will dictate how they care for patients. This is not true. Guidelines are there to ensure that everyone in the care process knows the best evidence-based practices for caring for common conditions. And process standardization is the only way to reveal and reduce variation. Rampant variation obscures our ability to see waste and error, to correct our processes, and care for patients. Physicians need to stress science over the art of medicine. Nothing can improve until processes are stabilized and then standardized. Only when processes are controlled can we work as a team to improve.[47]

Healthcare goals need to change. At present, various professional guidelines rate physicians and care as "excellent" if success rates hit 65% of one thing or 85% of another. An 85% success rate, however, still allows 150,000 defects per million opportunities. Infections and surgical errors should not be acceptable. Death is a natural consequence of living, but injury should not be an acceptable outcome of treatment. We need to reset our expectations to focus on zero as the right number. That means zero infections, zero errors, zero tragedies of our making. This is the only goal we should be aiming for, even if the patients in a provider's panel are "sicker" than the norm.

Physicians everywhere need to start thinking and talking to colleagues about payment and sharing resources so that the patient's health is the central focus. Doctors must negotiate with each other to decide who is paid what for treatment. Individual episodes of care will involve some types of physicians more intensely than others; nobody knows this

47. These statements are based on the work of W. Edwards Deming, a statistician, professor, and consultant of the 20th Century who shaped much of the underpinnings of lean thinking. All physicians should familiarize themselves with his work.

better than physicians. Rather than having insurers or hospital administrators or the government dictate how to split bundled payments, doctors need to get involved now, to begin building a payment system that makes sense. If physicians do not begin negotiations with one another now, someone else will be making these decisions.

Medical specialty societies should be leading or assisting public-reporting efforts. We need these societies to help develop consensus-driven measures, understandable to the public and truly reflective of quality outcomes within that specialty. Physicians who work with those societies need to push organizations to lead the efforts. Those that do not get involved early in these efforts may be forced to accept less-than-illuminative data regarding their work. Physicians need to ask if they want to define quality within their specialties or leave that to the federal government.

Next, physicians need to track their own quality and cost metrics, even if nobody else is looking. Quality metrics should be defined by a credible source such as The Wisconsin Collaborative for Healthcare Quality, or a medical specialty organization. Collecting cost data should be straightforward, but physicians rarely pay attention. As the United States moves toward bankruptcy, however, with medical bills being a major contributing factor, we no longer have the luxury of pretending that cost is someone else's concern.

Doctors who work in groups already tracking quality and cost need to understand what the data reveal about patient care, waste, and their own effectiveness. The next step is pushing that data out to the public. Our patients need and deserve factual reporting on medication errors, surgical infections, mortality rates, access to care, and cost. Everyone in healthcare should be examining the available data, asking whether it accurately reflects quality and cost outcomes in their field or specialty, and refining it where needed.

As healthcare providers, hospitals have unique issues. Mostly built for the benefit of communities and declared not-for-profit, many health-care organizations have entered a pitched competition, chasing the procedural dollar. In Wisconsin, as elsewhere, unnecessary hospitals have been built to expand a brand. A new 180-bed hospital built in Oshkosh, for instance, caused the census in the existing hospital to drop from averaging 100 patients a day to 50. The newer hospital, built for 180, had a similar fill rate. While competition is desirable, overcapacity is definitely not. Both organizations had to raise prices, either to pay for new construction or to cover the loss of revenue. It does not take a chief financial officer to add up the cost to the community, whose health bill just doubled without necessarily increasing quality levels. The total healthcare value in Oshkosh decreased significantly.

Instead of expanding brands and merging, hospital executives need to think about improving their value to the community. The goals should be increasing quality while *decreasing* prices—the opposite of what has been happening in the past 10 years. During my tenure as CEO of ThedaCare, the Board of Directors held the organization's price increases to the Consumer Price Index.[48] Most state hospital boards, however, allowed executives to raise hospital prices 10–15%, leading to a situation in which communities such as Milwaukee now have some of the costliest healthcare in the Midwest.[49] Hospital executives need to ask, how is this good for the community?

Like physicians, hospital administrators need to get actively involved in identifying and removing waste from care-delivery processes. Members of the Healthcare Value Network[50] have proved repeatedly that teams

---

48. For the 12-month period ending May 2011, for instance, the Consumer Price Index showed a 3.6% increase in prices for the nation.
49. In 2003, Milwaukee healthcare costs were 39% higher than other Midwest areas, according to a Mercer Health and Benefits study. By 2009, the disparity was reduced, but a study by Mercer and Milliman, commissioned by the Greater Milwaukee Business Foundation on Health, showed Milwaukee healthcare costs were still 8% higher than the Midwest average.
50. For more information about the Network go to www.createhealthcarevalue.com

working in hospitals can consistently remove 30–50% of wasted time, money, and energy from care processes.[51] It is appalling that more health-care leaders have not taken advantage of lean tools to improve operations.

Patients

Patients need to become forceful consumers of healthcare. During consultations with a physician, we all need to ask hard questions. The first and most consistent question is just four words that everyone needs to memorize: *Based on what evidence?* Patients need to ask about the underlying evidence for the diagnosis and if there are other inter-pretations. Once satisfied with the diagnosis, we need to ask for comparative outcomes for the proposed treatment.

This means Kathy Ceman would ask her physician for up-to-date information on how many knee replacements he performed, the percentage of infection or error during surgery, complications during the following three months for all patients, and his patients' recovery rate. She should also collect the same information from the hospital where the procedure is scheduled.[52]

If answers are not forthcoming, patients should walk away. When walking away is not possible, patients must politely demand the information. If the patient is incapacitated, family members must take on that role. If a physician is comfortable prescribing a course of treatment, he or she should be equally comfortable producing the data that shows the results of the treatment, as well at the scientific evidence that helped form the prescription. When possible—especially in the case of planned or elective procedures—every patient should be using the Internet to collect all information possible on the provider's quality outcomes and comparative costs.

---

51. Christina Bielaszka-DuVernay, "Redesigning Acute Care Processes In Wisconsin," *Health Affairs*, 30, no.3 (2011):422-425
52. Kathy Ceman's second knee-replacement surgery was without complications. She estimates that she was fully recovered after six or seven weeks and has been pain free since.

Asking these questions is not easy or comfortable for many people, and so they go unasked. In a system where someone else pays for treatment, patients are divorced from some very real issues in healthcare. Even on the question of quality, people often are too passive. This is why I believe that patients need to have skin in the game, in the form of choosing providers and at least partially paying for treatment, in order for the system to work.

Patients also need to take responsibility for their health decisions. With nearly one-third of all adults in the United States self-reporting as obese,[53] which is the underlying cause of most chronic ailments and some cancers, change in eating and exercise habits is imperative. We all belong to the same health system and it has limited resources and soaring costs. Therefore, every person owes it to his or her fellow citizens to take steps to avoid extra healthcare costs, such as not smoking, getting more exercise, and choosing better nutrition. Those who do not take steps to improve their own health should pay more into the healthcare system. Patients enrolled in Medicaid or other programs in which patients do not pay will be more challenging. Since 80% of all Americans are insured, we can assume that the 80/20 rule will apply and the majority of patients—who pay in part for healthcare and do not want to pay more—will exert pressure to change minds about patient responsibilities.

---

53. According to the Centers for Disease Control, 26.7% of adults reported a body mass index of 30 or greater in 2009. That figure has been steadily rising.

Payers

Payers fall into three broad categories: employers, insurance companies, and Medicare or Medicaid. Each of these groups controls different pieces of the data stream that must be combined in order to achieve transparency, and each has unique responsibilities in redesigning the system.

While each category of payer has distinct concerns and, perhaps, entirely different populations, their prescriptions are identical: Know what you are paying for, release your data to the public, and make payments in such a way as to improve healthcare value.

Employers have the most profound changes to make in approach simply because they have been laboring under the pretense that they are not part of the healthcare system. Sometime after World War II, employers abdicated their role in purchasing healthcare to insurance companies, telling insurers to go out and negotiate the best deals for employee medical care.

Insurers opened the healthcare menu and went after the line items, negotiating low prices on procedures. Employers liked getting those discounts and mostly failed to consider effects on the larger system. Take MRIs, for instance, which can be a large line item in any healthcare budget due to quantity. A health plan that offers a 50% discount on MRIs might look attractive, but that plan might also pay for multiple tests without regard to evidence-based guidelines, pay for knee-replacement surgeries that cost twice the regional average, and contract with every provider regardless of readmission rates. Saving 50% on MRIs in this case is no deal. In retail, those discount MRIs are known as "loss leader"—a possibly money-losing lure to get customers into a store. In healthcare, patients and employers end up trapped in high-priced stores where their wallets are drained.

Failure to drill down into the details and ask broader questions about the cost of healthcare has created myopia among employers. The cost has been enormous, with medical care for employees costing more than raw materials in many U.S. industries. Imagine if company executives bought the lowest-priced components for a product without asking how many components were needed, the parts' quality, or how those components affected the overall design and price of their product. Can you imagine a company like that surviving?

To become part of a solution that will rescue their own bottom lines, executives working for companies who are self-insured need to release administrative claims data into a qualified regional data source.[54] No matter how large the company, individual businesses just do not have the volume of procedures or healthcare episodes to make accurate judgments on quality and cost of providers based on their own records. Businesses need to join others in releasing this important data, stripped of patient identifying information. The data must attribute care to individual providers, allowing the comparison of provider performance. This information must be public, so that patients can actually see the cost of the services they receive.

Then, business leaders need to participate in conversations about value in healthcare and make decisions about how to pay for these big budget items in a way that produces improved outcomes at a lower cost.

Business leaders also need to track the health of their employees with Health Risk Assessments, as well as the company's efforts to encourage healthier habits. This sounds like a politically sensitive subject—with employers taking on the role of Big Brother, snatching cupcakes out of employee hands—but many companies already do this in order to secure lower insurance rates. John Torinus proved that employees

---

54. In most cases, only self-insured companies "own" their employee healthcare data, but all business leaders need to keep public reporting as a common goal.

would take advantage of a free annual physical, especially if the results could aid their overall health and lead to lower insurance co-pays. When patients were engaged—with skin in the game and information about quality and cost available—healthcare costs at Serigraph fell during a time when other companies saw increases of 10-15% a year. After contracting with ThedaCare to provide on-site clinics and annual Health Risk Assessments, Miller Electric enjoyed a 10% reduction in healthcare premiums and a return on investment of $2.52 for every dollar spent on an on-site nurse and part-time physician.

Companies that track employee health data and then make efforts to encourage better habits will have valuable information, over time, to help lower healthcare costs. But there is more to be done. Employers with 100 workers or more should seriously consider getting rid of the insurance-company model and contracting directly with the best value provider in the area. Businesses can work with an ASO (administrative services only) organization directly or another third-party administrator —such as a benefits design consultant—that has a proven process to identify the best value providers in the area. This might require cobbling together a system of multispecialty clinics and hospitals, but working out the details now is infinitely better for a company's future than continuing on, chasing medical-procedure discounts in an exhausting, expensive race to the bottom.

Insurance companies must release administrative claims data instead of saving it as a competitive advantage. Like businesses, insurance companies need to join efforts to create central data repositories that will be available to the public. This data does not belong in a corporate safe or in the lock box of a state insurance commissioner. Once scrubbed of individual identifiers and presented in a usable format, this data belongs to the public, to assist people in making better healthcare decisions. Public access to information on healthcare prices is as important as provider-quality data. Patients have been shielded from healthcare prices for too long. Seeing the cost of care will help to engage everyone in the issue.

Insurers are also in a unique position to radically change the system by rewarding providers who offer higher quality healthcare at lower cost. When insurers focus on the metrics that will truly move the needle, they can immediately affect the focus of healthcare providers. If insurers pay more for fewer hospital readmissions and offer bonuses for zero medication reconciliation errors, you can bet that physicians and hospitals will turn a laser focus onto those areas for improvement. Concentrating, as insurers have, on deep discounts for individual procedures too often means bigger bills for their business clients. (A fact that should make their clients angry.) Insurers that want to stay relevant should not wait for businesses to demand a change.

Insurers that want a pivotal role in healthcare's future should also invite providers to begin pilot payment-redesign projects. We need sizable experiments now on payment models such as global payment, shared savings, medical home, and bundled payments. Insurers should be helping to design and conduct these experiments in coordination with other insurers—as opposed to striking out on their own. Most insurers in Wisconsin, for instance, have agreed to participate in the Partnership for Healthcare Payment Reform. But a few large companies have opted for solo efforts, which I fear will damage the statewide payment reform initiative. We need focused, coherent trials. Providers can only handle so many different rule sets at once, and too many initiatives will muddy the results.

Please note that insurers and providers cannot directly address pricing, which could subject them to antitrust charges. Healthcare organizations should continue to negotiate prices privately with individual insurance companies. The important issue is not price, anyway. The critical work is developing an organized methodology for payment that rewards better health outcomes and pushes providers to deliver those better outcomes at lower cost.

Government payers such as Medicaid and Medicare need to work on openness. Currently, information that patients need is locked in government vaults, with strict rules that require any entity to get preapproval for use of the data. Medicare needs to release relevant claims data to regional, publicly reporting database initiatives as soon as possible, without attaching onerous costs. If the data are so expensive that only the big healthcare monopolies can afford to pay, the government will be undermining redesign efforts.

Most important, however, is the manner in which the data are released. As of this writing, the Centers for Medicare and Medicaid Services plans to release data in a manner of its choice, for a price. Qualified regional initiatives such as Wisconsin's all-claims database group, however, should not be charged for data intended for public use. Instead, Medicare employees should be working with regional initiatives to set up a continuing stream of relevant data, ensuring that this valuable information flows to those who need it most—everyone.

Government payers also need to focus on function, paying more attention to how payment affects healthcare. Medicare could be an important player in testing new payment systems around the country, but only if leaders stay focused on the prize. The goal should always be better health outcomes.

Medicare is an enormous power lever. If this payer adopted policies of transparency and patient-focused healthcare, we could move far and fast toward a more sustainable healthcare system. So far, it has been disappointing to see so little movement on releasing Medicare payment data and hence, payment redesign.

Building a Regional System

I am a strong advocate for building regional, multi-stakeholder collaboratives to create data collection and publishing initiatives because I know this model works. When payers, providers, policy-makers, and patient representatives sit down together to hash out issues, controversy is less likely to kill the initiative in infancy. There will be discord, of course. Uncomfortable questions will be raised and answered. But when all interested parties join the discussion, people try to find common ground. Actions can be proposed and agreed to; the work can move forward.

The goal of a collaborative is to develop a single methodology to collect and publish data. This will allow providers to follow a single set of rules, and to standardize data-collection processes. Focusing on a decrease in variation will help regional initiatives produce clear, usable information.

Leaders of a nascent initiative will have to do more than send out invitations to get started. Planning will help collaboratives begin on a professional tone.

A. Establish a start-up funding mechanism. In Wisconsin, the founding members each agreed to chip in $50,000 a year. Along with some government grants, that seed money kept the wheels on the bus for the first two years or so. As our numbers increased, we created two classes of membership—founders and subscribers. Newer members (subscribers) paid more for access to data. No matter what mechanism is chosen, make sure that money does not come with strings and conditions. The collaborative needs to be free to make choices as a natural outgrowth of discussions, without worrying about offending financiers.

B. Establish a multi-stakeholder governance board. No single category of stakeholder should dominate the governing board. Choose board members who can lead while achieving consensus. Avoid autocrats with separate agendas.

C. Create immediate goals to help kick-start an initiative. Every data-collecting collaborative should set deadlines to publish data, such as:
   1. Hospital readmission rates
   2. Complications during procedures
   3. Medication errors
   4. Infection
   5. Cost

Policy-makers

Policy-makers—meaning politicians, Congressional staff, government agency leaders, professors, think-tank lawyers, lobbyists, and anyone else who has a hand in crafting public policy—have focused their attention for too long on fine details such as funding mechanisms and process measures. It is time to broaden the scope to achieving better healthcare, first by collecting health outcomes measures, and publicly reporting quality and cost data. This is the only way we can form an accurate picture of healthcare.

To do this, policy-makers need to create legislation with a framework for reporting health outcomes, while leaving it to state collaboratives to determine the specifics. We need broad-outline laws forcing disclosure—such as specifying that these should be outcomes, not process measures—without getting into specific prescriptions that tie everyone in knots and invite lawsuits. Statewide or regional initiatives will be far more useful if they have flexibility to change as needs arise. If a region sees a sharp rise in obesity, for instance, or expensive procedures to fix common knee problems, the local initiative should be able to react quickly, collecting and publishing new data. Because the adage—we are what we measure—is true, specific measurements need to change dynamically with local circumstances.

Policy-makers should also encourage private-public initiatives in every region. Many states will need assistance—financial help and best-practices training—to get public reporting off the ground. I do not believe that states need complicated, exhaustive new policies dictating exactly how to launch these initiatives. We do not need regimentation. We need experimentation because no one person or ideological bent has exactly the right answer for an unwieldy healthcare system. Nothing puts a stranglehold on innovation faster than too much regulation.

Policy-makers also need to overhaul antitrust laws. Physicians and hospitals need to be able to work together for the good of the patient, without actually merging. There is a growing crisis of consolidation in the United States, which, if it continues, will leave patients without real choice. If antitrust laws more clearly allowed providers to work together without fear of conflicting with the law, mergers would seem unnecessary. It is up to lawmakers to preserve healthcare competition.

Finally, we need public education campaigns. Every adult needs to know how to compare physician and hospital performance on the elements that affect their families. This means knowing how many medication errors happened yesterday in the local hospital, as well as the five-year trend; how many infections and complications Dr. Smith had in the last 12 months; and the difference in cost between the two local hospitals, or between Dr. Smith and Dr. Jones. This should be as easy to read as food labels, and is certainly as important to everyone's health. The healthcare crisis in this country is a public health problem, like smoking or obesity or basic hygiene during flu season.

To combat rising costs and worsening health outcomes, we need an informed population. Then, we need benefit plans designed to make people care about cost and quality so that we can take an active role in our own future.

All of this is necessary because we have come to a point that change is inevitable. The country is on the verge of bankruptcy. The healthcare industry, after decades of growth, looks eerily akin to a bubble economy, like housing or technology. We have achieved revenue growth to the point that we are unaffordable.

After more than a decade spent studying the subject and conducting practical experiments with others, I believe that we finally have a diagnosis and a treatment plan to correct the situation.

The treatment plan I have offered here is not static. One never knows how a cure is working until it is studied. In all cases, the patient must be examined periodically during treatment and we must act on these findings. We must adapt constantly as we see how our very sick patient—better known as U.S. healthcare—responds to treatment.

The role I plan to play going forward is to collect findings and report on the outcomes of experiments, building the body of knowledge necessary to prescribe new and better treatments. Along with the ThedaCare Center for Healthcare Value, I have developed a website to serve as an information hub for the outcomes of experiments across the country. Go to www.createhealthcarevalue.com for more information.

We desperately need the common ground of a site like this, enabling everyone to see what we are discovering, share our experiment designs, and collaborate on the path forward. Much as a multidisciplinary care team collaborates to achieve the best outcome for the patient, so must employers, insurers, providers, and governments now work as a team. This will not be easy or natural, but it is the beginning of the cure.

End Note: How to Get Involved

By John Toussaint and Helen Zak

As the journey continues to create a U.S. healthcare industry that delivers improved value, we have been developing means for others to participate and learn how to improve the cost and quality of care delivery, create transparency of performance, and experiment with new models of payment. The ThedaCare Center for Healthcare Value has partnered with several organizations that have started this work.

The Center has formed the Healthcare Value Network (HVN) for healthcare providers to learn from peers who are transforming the delivery of care in their organizations using Lean methodology. The premise of the network is that participating organizations will be able to progress faster when collaborating with others. Organizations in the network have shown dramatic improvements in cost and quality of care through participation in various learning and sharing opportunities. These activities include on-site visits, sharing lessons learned on a collaborative private website, completing an assessment following the Shingo Prize principles (www.shingoprize.org), and participating in affinity groups to share knowledge in specific areas such as human resources and Lean process improvement. For more information and to apply for membership to the network, please visit the Center's website at www.createhealthcarevalue.com.

The Center also continues to work closely with the Lean Enterprise Institute (LEI). As a nonprofit education, publishing, research, and conference organization, LEI advances lean thinking throughout the world. LEI produces books, workbooks, educational events, and Lean summits. It has created a strong worldwide Lean community through its Lean Global Network, consisting of more than a dozen nonprofit organizations similar to LEI, sharing a common mission. To learn more visit the LEI website at www.lean.org.

The Wisconsin Health Information Organization (WHIO) is a voluntary initiative formed to improve the transparency, quality, and efficiency of healthcare. The organization is supported by visionary leaders from insurance companies, healthcare providers, major employers, and public agencies who share a commitment to the future of healthcare. WHIO has created one of the most comprehensive sources of health claims information available anywhere in the United States. Through its Health Analytics Exchange holding data for nearly 250 million claims for care provided to 4 million Wisconsin residents, WHIO offers unparalleled information for quality improvement. In addition the Center is working to develop a national health analytics exchange. This will require an even broader partnership with many organizations across the country. The goal will be the same as Wisconsin, however, which is to create a publicly available healthcare data set which can allow accurate quality and cost comparisons around the country. To learn more about WHIO go to www.wisconsinhealthinfo.org.

The Partnership for Healthcare Payment Reform (PHPR) is another voluntary initiative sponsored by WHIO to engage Wisconsin's diverse healthcare stakeholders in assessing, designing, testing, and implementing innovative comprehensive approaches to healthcare payment reform in order to improve the quality and affordability of healthcare. To learn more go to www.phprwi.com

Performance measurement and public reporting are vital, dual mechanisms for promoting greater transparency, improvement, efficiency, and equity within healthcare. The Wisconsin Collaborative for Healthcare Quality (WCHQ) is comprised of Wisconsin healthcare providers that voluntarily agree to share quality data on all patients in their practice. WCHQ releases a state-of-the-art, web-based, interactive "Performance and Progress Report" that allows any individual to access relevant, audited healthcare quality information, while comparing healthcare providers and performance measures. To see a report, go to www.wchq.org.

The ThedaCare Center for Healthcare Value invites all interested readers to share the outcomes of experiments and research. Visit the information hub at the Center's website (www.createhealthcarevalue.com) to learn how to report your experiment to the nation and learn from others. The hub will serve as a single place to collect these learnings from across the nation and build the collaborative path we need.

Acknowledgments

Our multi-stakeholder collaboration in Wisconsin has been the work of many outstanding leaders. Therefore, it is very difficult to name only certain individuals for fear of not giving credit to all, and since it took all of us to build the existing assets I want to recognize all present and former board members of the Wisconsin Health Information Organization and the Wisconsin Collaborative for Healthcare Quality. The boards had to make difficult decisions but these decisions have catapulted Wisconsin into a cutting-edge national leader in quality and cost data reporting.

There are a few individuals who have been there from the beginning and deserve recognition. From the insurer group, these include: Larry Rambo, CEO of Humana Wisconsin and Michigan; and John Foley, VP of Provider Engagement and Contracting, Blue Cross Blue Shield. From the government group, these include: Jim Doyle, the former Governor of Wisconsin; and two former Department of Health Services Secretaries, Helene Nelson and Karen Timberlake. From the provider group, these include: Don Logan, MD, former CMO of Dean Clinic; Fred Wesbrook, MD, former CEO of the Marshfield Clinic; Jeff Thompson, CEO of Gundersen Lutheran; and George Kerwin, CEO of Bellin Health. From the employer group, Dianne Kiehl, CEO of the Southeast Business Group on Health, and Mark Xistris, VP, Business Development and Provider Relations at The Alliance, brought the voice of the payer to the table.

It's also important to recognize the administrative leadership of WHIO and the WCHQ, which includes Julie Bartels and Chris Queram, respectively. In addition, Jo Musser, the former State Insurance Commissioner, was very helpful as a board member and subsequently as a staff member to WHIO. Little known is the many months of work Nancy Nankivil provided to get WHIO established when she worked for the state of Wisconsin Employee Trust Fund.

Her supervisor, Eric Stanchfield, "loaned" her to WHIO in a stroke of hope and genius. Kathy Franklin, an Organizational Development Specialist at ThedaCare, managed WCHQ for several months as we searched for the CEO position that Chris Queram eventually filled.

I also want to thank the CEO of the Wisconsin Medical Society, Susan Turney, MD, and VP Tim Bartholow, MD, as well as the Wisconsin Hospital Association CEO, Steve Brenton. Thanks also go to his many involved staff for providing significant leadership for many of Wisconsin's initiatives.

The Partnership for Healthcare Payment Reform leaders have included Dean Gruner, MD, CEO of ThedaCare and the leader of the acute-care initiative; Jim Riordan, CEO of WPS Insurance, the leader of the prevention initiative; and Mike Jaeger, MD, CMO of Anthem Wisconsin and leader of the chronic-disease initiative. There have been many other terrific physician and executive volunteers too numerous to list.

From ThedaCare, I would first like to thank our patients Nancy D'Agostino and Kathy Ceman, both of whom were willing to share their difficult stories to help us improve. In addition, primary care physicians Nate Grunwald, MD, and Monk Elmer, MD, helped us understand the coming changes from the primary care angle. On the specialty side Pulmonologist Jeff Whiteside, MD; Radiation Oncologist, Mike Ray, MD; and Oncologist and Palliative Care expert, Jack Swanson, MD, helped us understand the concerns of the specialty community. Many other ThedaCare staff helped on this project and I am very appreciative of their time and dedication.

I also received help from Jim Womack, Founder and Senior Adviser, Lean Enterprise Institute, as he poured over the manuscript looking for inconsistencies. Emily Adams brought the story to life with her brilliant written expression. Finally, my publisher Nancy Gurnee spent six months of her life making this work come to reality and for that I am truly grateful.

Index